DAILY DOSE

*A 90-Day Remedy to Encountering
a Fresh View of God*

TODD M DIEDRICH

WESTBOW®
PRESS
A DIVISION OF THOMAS NELSON
& ZONDERVAN

WestBow Press books may be ordered through booksellers or by contacting:

WestBow Press
A Division of Thomas Nelson & Zondervan
1663 Liberty Drive
Bloomington, IN 47403
www.westbowpress.com
1 (866) 928-1240

ISBN: 978-1-4908-8313-7 (sc)
ISBN: 978-1-4908-8314-4 (hc)
ISBN: 978-1-4908-8312-0 (e)

Library of Congress Control Number: 2015909050

Print information available on the last page.

WestBow Press rev. date: 7/29/2015

Contents

Introduction

Life is challenging, and each day brings new opportunities to allow God's grace to see you through. *Daily Dose* was written to bring you a daily message of God's peace for you. As you journey through life, my prayer is for you to take God with you and impact those you come in contact with for the kingdom of God.

Each devotional provides a Main Text of scripture that is the focal point of the day's reading. I encourage you to read the scriptures before and after the Main Text to gain a full appreciation of God's Word. The Meditation section is designed to challenge your day by focusing on a theme of inspiration and encouragement. Finally, you will close your devotional with a prayer of reflection and purpose. My hope is that *Daily Dose* will stimulate your daily walk with Christ. I trust you will be inspired and refreshed as you begin or end your day with a "dose" of God's Word.

Because of the LORD's great love we are not consumed, for his compassions never fail. They are new every morning; great is your faithfulness. —Lamentation 3:22–23

Todd

A Mighty Fortress

Main Text

2 Samuel 22:2–3: "He said: 'The LORD is my rock, my fortress and my deliverer; my God is my rock, in whom I take refuge, my shield and the horn of my salvation. He is my stronghold, my refuge and my savior—from violent people you save me.'"

Meditation

A few weeks ago when I stopped to visit my niece and her family, I was reminded of my own childhood. My niece has four children between the ages of one and ten. I call it the "Household That Never Sleeps" because there is some sort of action happening at every moment of the day. When I walked into the house, I knew what the activity of the hour entailed: fort building. You know what I am talking about— creating that secret hiding place where no stranger or danger could touch you. Blankets draped from chair to chair, from couch to the end table, from the television stand to the nail that once held the family picture on the wall, and pillows lined up in front of the entrance like guards. It was an incredible fort, one I would have been proud of as a child. The kids thought of every detail that made this a really cool fort.

I was impressed to see that fort building has survived in an era where electronic games and computers now reign as the primary source of kids' entertainment. As I stood there looking at this masterful structure of architecture, I was reminded of the words in 2 Samuel 22:2–3 that David penned after the Lord delivered him from his enemy Saul: "The LORD is my rock, my fortress and deliverer; my God is my rock, in whom I take refuge." God is certainly our refuge in times of trouble, a place we can run to and be safe. David recognized that it was the hand of God that delivered the victory over Saul and not anything that he did himself. God worked through David to be victorious over his enemy.

In our daily lives we need to do the same thing. We need to allow God access to our hearts to help us win the battles we face. We need to be willing to let God work in us and become the fortress we need in every situation. Too often, we think we have things under control and can fight the battle on our own. But when we think like this, we create unnecessary challenges and the victory will not be as sweet. Look to Jesus today to help bring victory in your life; He is the mighty Fortress and Deliverer.

Prayer

Jesus, You are my rock and fortress, my strength in time of trouble. Help me daily seek and trust You to bring victory in my life. Thank You, God, for being my heavenly Father. Amen.

Day 2

Fears and Phobias

Main Text

Isaiah 41:13: "For I am the LORD your God who takes hold of your right hand and says to you, Do not fear; I will help you."

Meditation

According to a recent survey, it is estimated that 19 million people suffer from one of 530 diagnosed phobias. A phobia is an excessive and irrational fear of something. The most common fears are the fear of spiders, or arachnophobia; the fear of snakes, or ophidiophobia; and the fear of heights, or acrophobia. If there is something to fear, there is a name for it.

Phobias are real and have many symptoms such as a pounding or racing heartbeat, shortness of breath, rapid speech, dry mouth, upset stomach, or even nausea. From time to time, I find myself staring in the face of a phobia. Take for instance the phobia trypanophobia, or the fear of injections. I am not a fan of injections, and I doubt many people enjoy them. If I had to guess, I would venture that many of us fall into the trypanophobia category.

When we fear something, it does not mean we need to be paralyzed by the event or circumstance. We have a greater Source that has overcome all fear: Jesus Christ. Isaiah 41:13 says, "For I am the LORD your God, who takes hold of your right hand and says to you, Do not fear; I will help you." I have stood on this promise many times in my life. It is the assurance given to us from God Himself that He will be there for us. He will hold our right hand and see us through whatever circumstances we face.

I encourage you today to reach out to Jesus; let Him hold your hand as you face the fears and phobias of the day. I assure you that He will not fail.

Prayer

Jesus, help me this day to overcome the trials that stand in my path. Let me hold tight to Your hand and lean on You to see me through this day. Thank You for your unyielding love and conquering my worries. Amen.

It's All About the Money

Main Text

Mark 12:42: "But a poor widow came and put in two very small copper coins, worth only a few cents."

Meditation

There are 180 currencies that are recognized as legal tender in the United Nations. Names like the Rupee, Dinar, Balboa, Euro, Ruble, and the US Dollar are a few that are included in the list of recognizable currencies from around the world. Money is part of every economy around the world and has been since the beginning of time.

The Bible speaks of money often, and Jesus Himself used many illustrations that relate to money. Jesus knew that money was an important aspect of life, and as a result, He often spoke about it. Money is not bad; in fact, money is good. It allows us to buy things we need and want like clothes, food, homes, and cars. Money allows us to help others in need, to feed children around the world, and to build schools and sport complexes.

Unfortunately, money can be used for bad purposes as well. Money contributes to crime, greed, envy, strife, and other unpleasant attitudes and things. Money has the ability to change people and their perspective. Take the illustration Jesus presented in Mark 12. Jesus watched as people brought their money and placed it into the temple treasury. Those with great wealth brought large sums of money and tossed it in the containers thinking nothing about where it came from or its potential. They simply gave because it was the thing to do. Then came the widow with only two small coins. She came to give her money out of a commitment to Jesus. Verse 44 tells us she "put in everything—all she had to live on."

I believe Jesus can use any money given for the advancement of His kingdom, regardless of the attitude of the giver. I do, however, believe that Jesus multiples and blesses our sacrificial giving. It isn't about how much we give, but rather the attitude in which we give.

Prayer

Father, take what I give and use it so that Your work may continue to touch hearts and lives around the world. Let me give sacrificially and with a cheerful heart. Amen.

Is Your Path Straight?

Main Text

Proverbs 3:6: "In all your ways submit to him, and he will make your paths straight."

Meditation

It was late Christmas Eve, and one of the largest and heaviest snowfalls of the early winter season struck. We had just finished opening Christmas presents at my family home and were ready to make the drive back to our house, which was about thirty minutes away. I remember walking out of the old family farmhouse that was so warm and inviting only to face a terrible snowstorm that had moved in quickly. As we left the farmhouse, it soon became apparent that the roads were in awful condition and there was little traffic on the highway. I remember blazing a trail through snow in our four-wheel drive vehicle where just several hours earlier the road was clear and visible.

As we drove through the thick, heavy, wet snow, we were filled with the fear of going into a ditch or skidding off the road because we couldn't see clearly where we were going. Although I had driven this road thousands of times, that night was a new challenge because the snow had created a road I had not experienced before. The snow continued to fall, and the conditions became worse. Driving that evening, I was reminded of Proverbs 3:5–6: "Trust in the LORD with all your heart and lean not on your own understanding; in all your ways submit to him, and he will make your paths straight."

Sometimes God takes us on a journey where we cannot see where we are going and He asks us to trust Him. Much like my Christmas

Eve snowstorm, often we can't see what's ahead and we have to rely on God to show us where to go. When we are faithful to Him, He is faithful to us, He guides us, and makes our path straight. Many times we don't understand where God is taking us and what He wants to do in our lives. In times like these, we need to trust Him and know that He is in control and will keep us safe.

Are you willing to trust Him for all your needs? Is your faith big enough to believe He will guide your steps and plan your route? Trust Him today for whatever you are going through. He does not fail!

Prayer

Father, I ask in Your name that You take me where You need me to go today. Give me the faith and courage to know You are in control of all things. I pray these things in the wonderful name of Jesus. Amen.

Stranded on a Deserted Island

Main Text

Romans 5:5: "And hope does not put us to shame, because God's love has been poured out into our hearts through the Holy Spirit, who has been given to us."

Meditation

Throughout the year I present at leadership conferences and facilitate strategic-planning sessions for businesses and organizations. One of the exercises I like to start my sessions with is asking the group a simple thought-provoking question, which always sparks a great deal of conversation. This question allows me to learn a lot about the participants' character in a very short period of time. Let's pretend for a moment that you are in one of my sessions and I ask, "If you were going to be deserted on an island all by yourself, what one item would you choose to take with you and why?"

I love the responses to this question. The things I have heard and the reasons behind them are always fascinating to me. A microwave, a photo of family, a comb, a Bible, matches, underwear, a pen . . . the list goes on. It comes down to taking something of value with you that will give you hope to endure. You see, it is not about the item itself as much as it is about what the item brings in terms of the individual's hope. Although some of the items seem silly and useless on a deserted island, the item helps the person hold on to the courage to continue looking forward.

While some comfort can be found in those objects, our ultimate hope is in Jesus Christ, who will rescue us from our pain, hurt, divorce, sickness, unemployment, or whatever the deserted island is that we are shipwrecked on. The beauty of our shipwrecked island is that we have a promised victory in Jesus Christ. In Romans 5:5, we read, "And hope does not put us to shame, because God's love has poured out into our hearts through the Holy Spirit, who has been given to us." What sweet assurance we have knowing we will be rescued as we keep our focus on Jesus Christ.

Put your trust in Jesus today. He will always be there to save you.

Prayer

Jesus, You are my hope in any circumstance I face. Even though I feel like I am stranded on a deserted island at times, I know that You bring unyielding faith to my heart as I trust in You. Thank You for freeing me. Amen.

Faithful God

Main Text

1 Corinthians 1:9: "God is faithful, who has called you into fellowship with his Son, Jesus Christ our Lord."

Meditation

Have your ever thought about the faithfulness of God? Have you been reminded that our God is faithful in the big and the small things? If you call, He will come. When you pray, He will hear. When you cry, He will dry your tears, because God is faithful. If you cast your cares into His arms, He will rescue you. You may not be able to see past the storm in front of you, but you can count on our faithful God.

Life is often challenging and filled with uncertainty. But there is one constant, one true source that remains unchanging and faithful: Jesus Christ. First Corinthians 1:9 states, "God is faithful." When life gets you down, when you are faced with pain, suffering, unemployment, death, or cancer—whatever the obstacle, we have a faithful God who is always interceding on our behalf. Jesus can never be defeated. He has overcome all things.

"I can't see past this storm, but I'm counting on a faithful God." We have a faithful Savior who has redeemed us and made us part of His family. Struggling today? Reach out to the Jesus, and He will be your unwavering guide.

Prayer

Father, You have created me and know me better than I know myself. I ask that You intercede this day and show Yourself a faithful God on my behalf. Shield me and protect me from what I may face. Amen.

Scatter the Seeds

Main Text

Mark 4:5: "Some [seeds] fell on rocky places, where it did not have much soil. It sprang up quickly, because the soil was shallow."

Meditation

I'm an old farm boy, born and raised on a dairy farm. When you live on a dairy farm, time does not belong to you. You are up early doing morning choirs and often working late into the night during harvest time. I really enjoyed the freedom and the experience of being raised on a farm. As I reflect on the experience now, though, I cannot say that I enjoyed every facet of my farm family heritage. One of the tasks that my siblings and I disliked above all other tasks was "picking rock" in the fields just before spring planting.

Picking rock is a dreadfully boring and never-ending task of clearing the fertile ground of any sizable rocks so that spring seed can be planted. If rocks were in the path of the seed planter, the seed would fall on top of the rock or be pushed under the rock. In either case, the seed fell to a spot where it could not grow. Year after year, the task of picking rock had to be done. I often wondered why there were always so many rocks on fields we planted every year. I am convinced now that it was God's way of creating a humble heart in me.

In Mark 4, Jesus taught His disciples using an illustration of a famer planting his crops to show them how His love is shared or planted in the lives of others. As the farmer planted his seeds, some of the seeds fell to rocky ground. These seeds quickly took root; however, when the heat of the sun touched the seedlings, they withered and died. When seeds were planted among thorns, the seeds also sprouted quickly, but soon were choked out by the tall thorns that hovered over the seedlings blocking the sunlight. The seeds that fell to fertile ground sprouted and produced a bountiful crop. So it is with us. We need to be open to God's will for our lives. We need to be willing to plant seeds where He wants and to fertilize those seeds with God's love.

Are you planting the seeds of Jesus' love in fertile ground that will help others grow in Christ? Or are you failing to plant seeds in the right spot by focusing on unhealthy or non-Christ-like actions? The choice is yours. Choose today to plant the seeds of God's grace in those you come in contact with. Where you plant Christ's love will determine what you yield. Are you planting in the right spots?

Prayer

Jesus, help me this day to plant Your love in the places You desire me to do so. Cause me to find fertile ground and make an impact for Your kingdom. Amen.

Eternal Home

Main Text

2 Corinthians 5:1: "For we know that if the earthly tent we live in is destroyed, we have a building from God, an eternal house in heaven, not built by human hands."

Meditation

I am not a handyman by any means; I neither have interest in nor talent to build things. God did not gift me with the skill to work with my hands. I will confess, however, that I am envious of those whom God has gifted with talents to build things. Over the past few weeks, my obvious deficiencies have been reinforced as a team of individuals and I have worked on a building project for our annual church mission's banquet.

Our goal was to build a small structure that resembled a Bible college dorm room. This room was to be used to demonstrate the meager conditions that Bible students live and study in as they attend Bible College in a third-world country. As our team was building the structure, I observed the meticulous details necessary to build even the simplest of structures. The measuring, cutting, squaring, nailing, gluing, and drilling . . . I think you get the picture. All of the things that I do not enjoy were talents this dedicated group of men and women had who built the dorm room. Not only were they good at it, but they enjoyed the building process and relished in the outcome of their labor.

As I watched the progress of the project from a distance, I could not help but be reminded of 2 Corinthians 5:1: "For we know that if the earthly tent we live in is destroyed, we have a building from God, an eternal house in heaven, not built by human hands." Although the structure we built served as an incredible backdrop for our mission's banquet, the real-life application is that Jesus has gone ahead and prepared for us our future home, one created specifically for us. You see, our eternal home in heaven was not built by human hands but has been built by the master builder Himself. Every detail of our everlasting home was designed and built by God, uniquely and perfectly for us.

Are you ready to go home? To your heavenly home, that is. If not, seek Jesus today and let Him restore you so you can be assured of your home not built by human hands but by those of God.

Prayer

God, You are the builder of my heavenly home. Thank You for the promises found in Your Word, that You have crafted an everlasting home in heaven with my name on the mailbox. Amen.

Day 9

Follow the Clouds

Main Text

Psalm 78:14: "He guided them with the cloud by day and with light from the fire all night."

Meditation

I like to start my day with a run to clear my mind, to get refreshed and recharged. While I was on one of my recent daily early-morning runs, I was reminded of God's great mercy and protection. As I ran, I happen to glance up at the sky as I was taking a deep breath and noticed a specific cloud that seemed to be leading me on my run. It felt odd, and something out of the ordinary that I had not experienced before. Immediately I was quickened to remember how God used a cloud to lead the Israelites on their journey toward the promised land. Psalm 78:14 says, "He guided them with the cloud by day and with light from the fire all night."

I pondered those words as I finished my run. You see, I believe God reveals to us each day the ways in which we should go and the ways that are best for us. The challenge is, will we be willing to accept God's leading? The cloud seemingly led me that morning, and I believe God placed that cloud in the sky specifically for me to recall His goodness, grace, and mercies that He has given me and to reassure me that He really is providing direction in my life. When we are obedient to Him and follow the path He has mapped for us, I am confident that He will lead us to the places we are to go. Are you willing to follow your cloud?

As you go throughout your day, remember to take a moment and look up. You may very well have a cloud waiting to lead you.

Prayer

Lead me this day, Father, to the place where You need me to go and cause me to experience You in a new way. Send Your cloud to guide me. Thank You, Jesus, for Your direction in my life. Amen.

Cookie Addiction

Main Text

Titus 2:11–12: "For the grace of God has appeared, bringing salvation for all people, training us to renounce ungodliness and worldly passions, and to live self-controlled, upright, and godly lives in the present age."

Meditation

I love cookies. Any kind of cookie: chocolate chip, oatmeal, molasses, cranberry, butterscotch. You name it, I will eat it. I tell my wife that I have never had a bad cookie. If there were a Cookie Anonymous Club, I'd be the president of the organization. As silly as this sounds, it is true. If you are honest with yourself, you too have some sort of addiction you simply cannot break. Perhaps it's watching television, spending too much time surfing the web, excessive exercising, overeating. Whatever your addiction, it's a hard cycle to break. Sometimes I eat too many, but I cannot stop myself. You too may find yourself in the "but I cannot stop myself" phase of your compulsion.

Unfortunately, we all have those vices in life that we know we need to control but find it hard to do. Titus 2 speaks of God's grace and mercy toward us. If we seek God and ask Him to help us, He is gracious to do so. Grace is God showing us His love even though we may not deserve it. We cannot earn God's grace; it is something He freely gives us. When God imparts His grace to us, we must be willing to accept it as a gift. The gift God gives us is eternal life if we are willing to accept it. When we fall, God is there to pick us up. When we fail, God is there to carry us. When we disobey, God is there to forgive us. Whatever your addiction or sin is, you are redeemed by God's grace.

Reach out to God today and receive His gift of immeasurable grace. When we reach out to God, He stands willing to accept us for who we are and the baggage we carry. Take God at His word; you won't regret it.

Prayer

Father, Your grace is sufficient for me, just as Your Word declares. Let me accept Your gift and share it with others. Amen.

Day 11

Fall Is in the Air

Scripture

Matthew 6:26: "Look at the birds of the air; they do not sow or reap or store away in barns, and yet your heavenly Father feeds them. Are you not much more valuable than they?"

Meditation

You can tell fall is in the air when the wild turkeys return. Not just a few wild turkeys, but large flocks of forty or more birds. Our home is surrounded on all sides by large trees that shelter our house and make it a haven of sorts for all kinds of animals and wildlife. As the seasons change, so do the animals that make our house their home.

Each fall I become a wildlife game watcher. I scout for the wild turkeys as they begin their annual fall migration to our backyard. Imagine with me for just a moment the scene as forty wild turkeys descend upon my backyard. It is quite a sight, and sometimes comical to watch as the game of turkey against turkey takes place to see which turkey gets to eat out of the bird feeder first. One of my personal favorite turkey games is what I have named the turkey trot. What is the turkey trot? Plain and simple, it is a single file line of forty turkeys marching in perfect formation as if they were soldiers. They strut their stuff all the way around the house marking their territory. It is fun to watch their crazy maneuvers and the turkey games they plan. Although my wife is not very fond of the turkey droppings they leave all across the yard.

As I sat in our sunroom and watched the turkey traffic march by the windows, I was reminded of Matthew 6:26: "Look at the birds of the air; they do not sow or reap or store away in barns, and yet your heavenly Father feeds them. Are you not much more valuable than they?" Jesus told us that we are of great value to Him, so much so that He takes time to remind us of His protection and provision in our lives. The turkeys have little concern for what they will eat and who will take care of them during the winter.

I pondered this principle as I thought about the worries we face daily. Are we not more valuable to God than the birds of the air or the silly turkeys that strut around my backyard? We are created in God's workmanship, made for His glory. Let us marvel in the fact that we are God's valued children and that He loves us so much that He gave His Son's life specifically for us.

This fall season, when you see flocks of wild turkeys, think about the verse in Matthew 6 that reaffirms the love God shows us and thank Him for His grace that has set us free.

Prayer

God, thank You that You value me and that You love me for who I am. Let me always seek You and leave my burdens in Your hands. Amen.

Laundry Day . . . Again

Main Text

Psalm 51:10: "Create in me a pure heart, O God, and renew a steadfast spirit within me."

Meditation

I don't know about your household, but in our house, the laundry is a never-ending chore. It seems the laundry basket is always full. I must confess, I dislike doing laundry—a lot. I realize that there are not many people who actually enjoy doing laundry, but when I say I dislike doing laundry, I mean I *really* dislike doing the laundry. I will find any excuse possible to avoid this chore. Laundry to me is one of those tasks that have no practical purpose. You wash something, wear it once, and the cycle starts all over. I am convinced there has to be a better way.

As I recently stood staring at three large mounds of laundry neatly piled in the laundry room, I took a deep sigh, rolled up my sleeves, and began the task. I am not so much opposed to the washing machine part of the task as I am to the drying, folding, and ironing stage—that's where I stumble. Knee-deep in laundry, I was reminded of Psalm 51:10: "[Create] in me a pure heart." I am not sure why God caused this verse to come to my mind in the middle of laundry day, but He did. As I thought about this verse, it occurred to me that God did create in me a clean heart and He renewed in me a right and steadfast spirit. You see, God has cleansed my heart and forgiven me. He has created in me a steadfast spirit, and I can reside in God's presence as I strive to live according to His ways.

Living a steadfast life is not easy. You must constantly seek God and His plan for your life. As your King, ask Him what He would have for you. Then you need to be willing to trust that God's way is best and rely on Him. Has God cleansed you? Has God created in you a steadfast spirit? If not, seek God today and ask Him to make your heart clean.

Prayer

Father, You are almighty, the only God who can cleanse me and make a right spirit in me. Forgive me this day and prepare me as I go about my daily work. Thank You for Your gift of everlasting life. Amen.

The Crown

Main Text

James 1:12: "Blessed is the one who perseveres under trial because, having stood the test, that person will receive the crown of life that the Lord has promised to those who love him."

Meditation

I know very little about horses and never had a desire to be around them or learn about them. My brother-in-law loves horses and has a fascination with Arabians. As a child he took riding lessons, attended special training courses, and competed in local horse shows. Over the years his passion continued to grow so much so that he now owns several Arabian horses and trains with them daily.

Not long ago, my brother-in-law invited me to attend a horse show where one of his horses was competing. Despite my initial lack of interest, with a bit of prompting from my wife, I agreed to go. I was amazed by the beauty, control, and presence of these magnificent animals. They were poised and obedient, doing exactly as their handlers instructed them. Each step was graceful as if rehearsed over and over until the steps were perfect. I was amazed at the work and dedication that went into training these animals to possibly win the prize, the victor's crown.

James 1:12 came to mind as I watched my brother-in-law's Arabian take the champion's crown at the show: "That person will receive the crown of life that the Lord has promised to those who love him."

How often in life do we face challenges that test us? When we persevere and remain steadfast, we are assured of taking the prize that

Jesus has pledged to us: eternal life. Just like my brother-in-law's horse that won the champion's crown, our reward awaits when we are faithful, obedient, and finish our competition called life.

Be steadfast and unmovable in your walk with Jesus Christ today. Your crown awaits.

Prayer

Father, help me this day to stay focused on You and serve You. Let me keep my eye on the gift of the crown of life as promised in Your Word. Amen.

You Can Set Your Clock

Main Text

2 Thessalonians 3:3: "But the Lord is faithful, and he will strengthen you and protect you from the evil one."

Meditation

If you have ever had the opportunity to visit Yellowstone National Park in Wyoming, you have more than likely been privileged to see Old Faithful. Old Faithful, named in 1870 during the Washburn-Langford-Doane Expedition, was the very first geyser named in Yellowstone National Park. You can set your watch by Old Faithful, which will erupt every ninety-one minutes, shooting boiling water into the air an average of 106 to 185 feet. It is a fascinating sight to stand on the viewing platform and experience the faithfulness of this nearly 150-year-old discovery.

We have a heavenly Father who is also faithful in all He does and says. God is faithful in meeting our needs, healing our bodies, and providing for our physical and mental needs. God leads, directs, and takes us to the places He needs us to go. When we are faithful to God, God is faithful to us. Remember times in your life when God showed His faithfulness to you. Did He keep you safe in a time of turmoil? Did He touch your body when you were ill? Did He meet your financial need when you thought there were no options? In all of these situations and more, God proved Himself faithful.

You are a living testimony to God's faithfulness. Tell someone today about how God met your need. Encourage those in need to look to God for help. He will be faithful to them too. Rejoice today in knowing that in an even more precise and everlasting way, God is like Old Faithful in being timely when we need Him most.

Prayer

Father, thank You for Your promise to me, even though I do not deserve it. You are an amazing God and I love You for Your steadfast, unfailing grace. Amen.

Day 15

Kings and Queens

Main Text

Revelation 21:18: "The wall was built of jasper, and the city of pure gold, as pure as crystal."

Meditation

They're mentioned in news shows, splashed across magazine covers, and watched by professionals assigned to report their every move. Royals. We're fascinated by royalty. Who are the kings and queens of countries around the world? What recent news events touched their lives? We hang on to their every word and action. Those glimpses help us live brief royal moments vicariously through them.

For most of us, the best we can do is to live the royal dream through those on the throne. But wait, is this true? The Bible declares we are children of the King of kings, Jesus Christ. This makes us royalty. Have you thought about the fact that you are royalty? It's true. Jesus Christ has called us to be royalty and to live a life of honor to our King.

Unlike kings, queens, princesses, and princes of the world, we are true blood relatives of the King of kings, Jesus Christ. Revelation 21:18–21 states that heaven has streets of gold that are as clear as glass and walls covered in precious stones and gems. Think about the beauty and the magnitude of castles for the royal families around the world. We marvel at the size and splendor of the homes of these kings, queens, and royal families. But I am pretty sure that most royal families are not walking on streets of gold. Heaven is far greater than any earthly palace.

I can't wait to see what my castle looks like in heaven. As I think about the magnitude of my King, I am confident that I will not be disappointed in what my "digs" will look like in heaven. The next time you hear news about a royal family, know that your royal status trumps their status hands down.

Prayer

King Jesus, You are my King. I bow before You this day with praise and honor of who You are and what You stand for. I know that I am part of Your royal family. Thank You for Your grace and mercy that give me hope in seeing You in heaven someday very soon. Amen.

Water Walker

Main Text

Matthew 14:25–26: "Shortly before dawn Jesus went out to them, walking on the lake. When the disciples saw him walking on the lake, they were terrified. 'It's a ghost,' they said, and cried out in fear."

Meditation

How many of the miracles Jesus performed in the gospels can you name? There's the healing of two blind men, the healing of a mute, the coin in the mouth of a fish, the healing of a deaf and mute man, the miraculous catch of fish, the raising of the widow's son, and more. The gospels record thirty-seven different miracles of Jesus, thirty-eight if you count His resurrection, including, healings, calming storms, walking on water, turning water into wine, and raising people from the dead. All in all, it's a very impressive resume, wouldn't you say?

Jesus is a miracle-producing Savior who can move mountains and set captives free. As I read the Scriptures and focus on the miracles found in the Gospels, I cannot help but come back to the miracle of Jesus walking on water in Matthew 14. Think about this wildly unthinkable feat: a man physically walking on water and not sinking. The thought of this act is simply inconceivable to me.

Matthew 14:25 says, "Jesus went out to them, walking on the lake." I believe I am intrigued by this miracle so much because I am not fond of water; in fact, I am afraid of water and do not enjoy being around water. To think that a person can actually walk on water blows my mind. I marvel at all the miracles Jesus performed. Each miracle was an act of doing something that no one else could. They were all impossible, unthinkable, unimaginable, and mind-blowing acts of a single man, a Savior and King we call Jesus Christ.

The next time you believe something to be impossible, read a miracle from the Gospels. I can promise it will change your life.

Prayer

Jesus, You are the miracle-working King who walked on water, healed blind eyes, and made deaf ears hear. Help me recognize miracles You are working in my life, and draw me into a deeper knowledge of You. Thank You, Jesus, for Your miraculous gift of salvation to me. Amen.

City Fortress

Main Text

Isaiah 12:2: "Surely God is my salvation; I will trust and not be afraid. The LORD, the LORD himself, is my strength and my defense; he has become my salvation."

Meditation

I remember building forts with my brothers as a child. Hours and days would pass as we worked on building a fortress that could not be attacked—at least by our sister. We would take any scrap material we could get our hands on and nail, staple, glue, and tape it together to build our "secret fort." What an awesome memory, one that is shared by many young children around the world.

Recently I had the opportunity to study the city of Rothenburg, Germany. Rothenburg is a walled city dating back to 1274. It's surrounded on three sides by very steep and almost insurmountable terrain, making access to the city limited to one main entry point.

Perhaps more legend than story, it is said that Rothenburg survived for nearly thirty-five years without an enemy penetrating its walls. The day came, however, when Rothenburg found itself under attack and the city was captured. It is reported that a human error was the culprit that cost Rothenburg its freedom. While under attack, a guard was asked to check the supply of gunpowder in the storage tower. In what would become a regrettable lapse of common sense, the guard lit a torch and entered the tower, leaving another guard to stand watch outside. Gunpowder. Fire. An explosive combination.

How often do we fail because of human error? We take our eyes off our guard, Jesus Christ. We get busy with life and become careless, letting the enemy attack our walled city, our heart. God's Word declares that we are to place our trust in Him and not be afraid.

Today as you go through your day, remember to guard your heart with wisdom and common sense by the power of Jesus' name.

Prayer

Father, You are my fortress and strength, and You are worthy of all of my praise. Thank You for Your protection and guidance. I ask that You protect me this day and guard my heart. I love You, Jesus. Amen.

Day 18

Hands and Feet

Main Text

Colossians 3:23: "Whatever you do, work at it with all your heart, as working for the Lord, not for human masters."

Meditation

Have you ever thought about your hands and feet? Your feet carry you where you need to go. You can walk, run, skip, and jump. Your hands lift, carry, point, bend, twist, and pivot. The human foot has twenty-six bones while the hand has twenty-seven bones. I am always amazed at how intricate God made us; He thought of every detail.

Although the Creator designed our hands and feet for functionality, Christ used an analogy in Scripture that we are to be the hands and feet of Jesus. By this, Jesus intended us to serve and minister to others. In fact, we can find in the Bible many examples Jesus provided for us to show us how we are to serve others. Remember the parable of the good Samaritan who cared for a stranger alongside the road (Luke 10:25–37)? The Samaritan helped this man in several ways by tending to him physically as well as paying for the cost of his care. Quite easily, the good Samaritan could have walked right by the man, just as others before him had done. But there was something different about the good Samaritan that caused him to stop and serve.

Jesus called each of us to serve Him by helping others. In other words, by being His hands and feet. Does your neighbor need help mowing their lawn or shoveling snow? Does a stranger alongside the road need a meal? Can you be a friend to the friendless? Can you serve when no one else is able or willing? Can you give financially to meet a need?

The hands and feet of Jesus know no limits and have no rules. Each of us sees things differently and each of us may be inspired to help serve in different roles and capacities. The next time you see a need, be the hands and the feet of Jesus by serving. I can promise you the blessing will be more yours as the giver than that of the receiver.

Prayer

Jesus, thank You that You gave me the example to be Your hands and feet. Cause me to give unconditionally as You would. Bless those I serve in Your name. Amen.

At the Sound of the Trumpet

Main Text

Joshua 6:5: "When you hear them sound a long blast on the trumpets, have the whole army give a loud shout; then the wall of the city will collapse and the army will go up, everyone straight in."

Meditation

The United States is a major military force with five specific branches all designed to protect its shores. The US Armed Forces includes the Air Force, Army, Coast Guard, Marine Corps, and Navy. Each division of the armed forces specializes in tactics and maneuvers that make them uniquely qualified to defend and protect the United States. The technology and weaponry are sophisticated and complex and require precise, rigorous training. Continuous training exercises and conditioning of enlistees are necessary in order to be ready at a moment's notice when and if they are called to duty by our commander in chief.

There was another commander in chief that did not have such specialized weapons or advanced training that captured an entire city by the mere act of obedience. God used Joshua, the son of Nun, to bring down the walls of Jericho. The story in Joshua 6 goes like this: Joshua was leading the Israelites when they came to the city of Jericho. Jericho was a walled city that was designed to the keep the enemy out and its citizens in. The Lord promised Joshua that if he would follow His simple battle plan, He would provide a way to seize the city. The battle plan included specific activities that the Lord gave to Joshua. There were four simple instructions. First, Joshua was to take his army and march once around the wall of Jericho for six days in a row. Second, seven priests were to carry their rams' horns in front of the ark as they marched with Joshua's army. Third, on the seventh day, the army, the priests, and the ark were to lap Jericho seven times with the priests blowing their horns. Fourth, on the last lap on day seven, Joshua's entire army was to give a loud shout. Sounds ridiculous, but we know the outcome of this story. After following these four simple steps, the walls of Jericho collapsed and the army captured the entire city of Jericho. Victory!

Sophisticated weapons, no. Trained military intelligence, no. Advanced battle plan, no. Hand of the Lord, yes. This is documented proof that when the Lord gives direction, we can be sure of the outcome He promised. Although His tactics may be unconventional, His victory is sweet. Are you willing to submit to an unconventional battle plan and place your trust in Jesus? Sound the ram's horn, for your victory is nigh.

Prayer

Father, Your victory is sweet when I look to You and trust. Although I may not understand Your plan, You provide victory by my obedience to You. Thank You for Your victorious power in my life. Amen.

Is That Tall or Is That Short?

Main Text

1 Samuel 17:4: "A champion named Goliath, who was from Gath, came out of the Philistine camp. His height was six cubits and a span."

Meditation

I was listening to the early-morning news recently when the news anchor caught my attention by stating that the world's tallest living man and the world's shortest living man had recently met. Standing at a towering eight foot three, Sultan Kösen met the small one-foot-nine-and-a-half Chandra Dangi, both, by the way, Guinness Book of World Record holders for their heights. As I watched the astonishing footage, I was fascinated by how vastly different two people could be in height.

The Bible story of David and Goliath in 1 Samuel 17 is spectacular to me. I always like to cheer for the underdog in any competition. I guess it makes me feel good knowing that someone of lessor skill, size, or means can come out with a victory.

When I read about David and Goliath, I imagine the huge hulking giant named Goliath standing on the field awaiting his opponent, David, who likely measured in at five feet six inches (average estimated height for that time). Goliath's height was recorded in verse 4 as "six cubits and a span." Bible Apologetics estimates this to be nine feet six inches tall. I wonder if Goliath had a problem finding pants that were long enough.

With the difference in size, one would immediately conclude that Goliath would be the champion of the match. But wait, there's more to it than physical size. Scripture reports that David came against Goliath in the name of the Lord Almighty, which in "short" means David would win.

When you read about how David came against Goliath in the name of the Lord Almighty, there is no denying that there was and still is power and victory in the name of the Lord. Whatever your giant may be, know there is victory when you call on Jesus. Even if the competition seems unbelievable, the power of Jesus' name brings triumph.

Prayer

Jesus, Your name is mighty and powerful, and through Your name, I have victory in all things. Today I give You praise for victories that are mine through Your almighty name. Amen.

Day 21

Refreshing Drink

Main Text

John 4:7: "When a Samaritan woman came to draw water, Jesus said to her, 'Will you give me a drink?'"

Meditation

Did you know that 71 percent of the earth's surface is covered by water? Or that the average American family uses four hundred gallons of water per day? Think about these statistics for just a moment. It's incredible to think how necessary water is to our everyday life and yet we take it for granted, assuming it will always be there. Although we may thirst from a physical perspective, we can be assured that we have a source that can quench our spiritual need.

Traveling from Jerusalem in the south to Galilee, Jesus and His disciples took the shortest route, through Samaria. Tired and thirsty, Jesus sat by Jacob's Well while His disciples went into the village of Sychar, which was about a half mile away. They planned to buy food and supplies for their trip. In the hottest part of the day, mid-day, a Samaritan woman came to the well to draw water. There the Samaritan women found Jesus sitting, waiting for the disciples to return. Little did the Samaritan woman know that her life was about to change. Jesus engaged the Samaritan woman in conversation and asked her to draw water for Him to quench His thirst. In exchange, Jesus presented the Samaritan woman with the opportunity to have eternal life for her soul and drink of water that is eternal.

Our bodies are comprised of 65 percent water. It is estimated that we can live no longer than three to five days without water. We have the promise, however, that we can have eternal life that is found in Jesus Christ. Have you taken the drink of eternal life? If not, seek Jesus today. He is sitting by the well, waiting for you.

Prayer

Father, You are the giver of life and the one who freely quenches my thirst. Let me drink from Your everlasting well today and know You in a personal way. Thank You for giving me eternal life where I will never thirst again. Amen.

The Hem of His Garment

Main Text

Luke 8:45–46: "'Who touched me?' Jesus asked. When they all denied it, Peter said, 'Master, the people are crowding and pressing against you.' But Jesus said, 'Someone touched me; I know that power has gone out from me.'"

Meditation

The Bible tells us, that Jesus is the divine healer and can meet our physical needs in an instant if we simply believe. As I think about Jesus as our healer, I recalled a recent news article I read about medical treatments. The article stated that new doctors were on average spending eight minutes with each patient during the course of their day. Imagine an eight-minute appointment with your doctor to diagnose, treat, and counsel you on your health.

One of my favorite stories in the Bible is the lady who touched the hem of Jesus' garment and was instantly healed (Luke 8:40–48). What is so significant about the hem of Jesus' garment? The word *hem* actually refers to the fringes, or tassels (called *tzitziyot* in Hebrew) that were required to be on the four corners of all clothing of Jewish men. These tassels dangled at the four corners of a man's garment to remind Jewish men of their responsibility to fulfill God's commands.

Suppose for just a moment you were this woman who had been sick for twelve years and imagine all of the medical treatments you tried that had failed. In desperation, this woman fashioned a plan to have an encounter with Jesus. However, she wasn't seeking to speak with Jesus or even to let Him know she was there. Her plan was simple and quiet; she just wanted to touch "the edge of his cloak" (v. 44). I believe in her mind she thought Jesus was so powerful that if she could just touch the tassel of His garment then she would be healed. My friend, that is unbridled faith. Scripture tells us that this woman was successful in touching Jesus' hem. So successful, in fact, that Jesus stopped His activity and posed the question, "Who touched me?" (v. 45). Embarrassed and trembling, the women fell at Jesus' feet and began telling Him her story. Her simple and unwavering faith caused her to be healed because she believed. Did you read that? Because she believed.

Do you need to touch the hem of His garment today? Reach out in faith, trusting as this woman did that the simple touch to the hem of His garment can make you whole. Believe today.

Prayer

Father, You are the divine healer. I ask this day that Your healing virtue would touch my body and make me whole. Give me the faith to simply touch the hem of Your garment and trust You for my needs. Amen.

Day 23

Oh Death, Where Is Thy Sting?

Main Text

Philippians 1:21: "For to me, to live is Christ and to die is gain."

Meditation

From 1933 to 1943 it is reported that eleven thousand Jews and German nationals not committed to Hitler's movement died at the Dachau Concentration Camp outside of Munich, Germany. The conditions at the camp were inhuman. People were mistreated in uncountable ways. Beatings, starvation, public humiliation, and torture were commonplace for those who had the misfortune of having to call Dachau their home.

As I walked the grounds of Dachau, I was overcome with emotion of what these eleven thousand people endured on a daily basis. I imagined in my mind the devastation and hurt that was experienced during these years. I began to pray, not for those whose lives were taken, but for those who do not know Jesus Christ as their Savior.

Philippians 1:21 says, "For to me, to live is Christ, and to die is gain." As sobering as Dachau Concentration Camp is, and the impact it made on me, I am reminded of the good news that belongs to each of us. The good news is that Jesus Christ does hear our prayers, answers our cries, and saves our hearts. Life is difficult, and unfortunately we face too many life crises that bring hurt, pain, and yes, even death. However, we can be assured that someday death will be wiped away, tears will be dried, and a newness will be revealed to those who trust in Jesus. Although we remember the hurt of the past, we have the blessed assurance of a glorious future.

Prayer

God, life is full of hurt and pain, and although I know You allow things to happen in my life for a reason, I ask that You remove the hurt and let me focus my attention fully on You. Grant me this day a new fullness of who You are. In Your precious name I pray. Amen.

Day 24

Tell It to Jesus

Main Text

Philippians 4:6: "Do not be anxious about anything, but in every situation, by prayer and petition, with thanksgiving, present your requests to God."

Meditation

Think about the evolution of the world's communication in the last 150 years. First came the pony express, then the telegraph, telephone, mail, fax, computer, e-mail, text message, instant messaging, and now live video chat that takes you around the world with a few clicks of your computer's keyboard. Who would have thought that our world would have evolved so quickly in such a short period of time?

It is estimated that every day 183 billion e-mails are sent and received while an average of 12 billion text messages are sent and received worldwide. That's a lot of communication daily considering our world population is approximately 7 billion people. Makes me wonder what 7 billion people have to say to each other.

Our world is immersed with communication. We desire to stay connected with family and friends and share with them the events of our lives. Jesus Christ also desires to stay in communication with us. In fact, Philippians 4:6 tells us, "Do not be anxious about anything, but in every situation, by prayer and petition, with thanksgiving, present your requests to God." In other words, communicate with Jesus and tell Him what is happening in your life. Jesus desires to stay connected with you as you share with Him your needs, offer your praise, and rejoice in His goodness through prayer. Prayer is the form of communication we use to share our life with Him.

Are you spending time communicating with Jesus? Reach out to Him in prayer today and present your requests and praise to Him. Jesus' inbox is never too full to accept your prayer. Tell it to Jesus today.

Prayer

Thank You, Jesus, that You are never too busy to accept my prayers. I know that You desire to hear from me and to communicate with me through Your Word. Help me not neglect talking to You daily. Amen.

Day 25

Hey, Mom

Main Text

Exodus 2:7: "Then his sister asked Pharaoh's daughter, 'Shall I go and get one of the Hebrew women to nurse the baby for you?'"

Meditation

How many famous moms can you name? *Leave it to Beaver's* mom, Jacqueline Kennedy, Princess Diana, to name just a few. Moms are definitely an influential member of most families; they act as caregivers, taxi drivers, financial advisors, cooks, counselors, and doctors. The list of a mother's duty never ends.

Jochebed, meaning "glory of Jehovah," was no exception to the definition of *mom*. Jochebed, was a Hebrew slave and the mother of Aaron, Miriam, and Moses. Quite an all-star cast of biblical children, wouldn't you say? Although Jochebed was foremost a mother to her family, Scripture portrays her as much more. Jochebed was a risk taker, an extreme risk taker in my opinion. When Moses was born, there was a decree that mandated all male children were to be killed upon birth. Jochebed defied the law and hid Moses for the first three months after his birth. Then she wove a basket, placed Moses in the basket, and put the basket in a nearby river. Not only did Jochebed risk Moses' life by this stunt, but also hers and her daughter Miriam's. Jochebed gave Miriam instructions to watch the baby in the basket to ensure his safety.

You know the rest of the story (Exodus 2:1–10). Low and behold, the miraculous occurred. Baby Moses ended up in the hands of royalty, and Jochebed was summoned to care for him. Moses grew up, and God used him to change the direction of all mankind. Ponder for a moment the ramifications of Jochebed's action. What if she had not risked it all, including her child and her very own life? What if she had not flirted with danger? What if . . .?

God calls each of us to be risk takers for Him, to make an impact, to change our community, city, state, nation, or perhaps even the world. Are you ready to risk it all for the sake of the call?

Prayer

God, You are the supreme risk taker. You gave Your life to give me life eternal. In return, cause me to be the risk taker You need me to be. Amen.

Superheroes

Main Text

Ephesians 1:19: "And his incomparably great power for us who believe. That power is the same as his mighty strength."

Meditation

If I were to ask you who your favorite cartoon superhero is, I would guess it would conjure up memories from your childhood. Children love the most current and hip superhero with laser guns, electronic gadgets, and superpowers that can make them fly, twirl, and speed to the scene of those in need in an instant. A recent poll I read ranked the top ten superheroes of all time. Can you guess who they are? Starting at number five, Wonder Woman, Superman, Wolverine, Spiderman, and the number one superhero of all time: Batman. Pretty impressive lineup of superheroes, isn't it?

Batman originally appeared in May of 1939, in Detective Comics #27. Batman is the secret identity of Bruce Wayne, an American billionaire, industrialist, and philanthropist. Unlike most superheroes, Batman does not possess any superpowers; instead, he makes use of his intellect, detective skills, science and technology, wealth, physical strength, martial arts skills, and tactfulness in his quest to fight crime. Batman wins based on his skill and defeats the enemy. In every show ever written, Batman comes out on top in the end. The crime is stopped, the enemy is defeated—end of story.

I don't know about you, but there are days when I wish I had the superhero skill and ability to leap a building in a single bound or flip a car over with one arm. But there is a power that is even greater.

Ephesians says that we have the power of Jesus Christ in our lives if we simply believe in Him. You see, all authority and power are given to us by Christ's death and resurrection at Calvary. How often we forget that our true strength and power come from the Creator of heaven and earth. We have the true source of all authority and power in Jesus' name when we accept Him in our life.

Do not spend a single day without the influence and direction of Jesus Christ. He is our salvation and deliverer in time of need. Call upon Him today; He will be there in a flash.

Prayer

Father, You are my true superhero. You protect, guide, guard, help, direct, and give purpose in my life. You are the supreme source of victory. Give me the power needed today to serve You. Amen.

Day 27

Perseverance Prevails

Main Text

1 Corinthians 9:24: "Do you not know that in a race all the runners run, but only one gets the prize? Run in such a way as to get the prize."

Meditation

Perseverance is defined as a steady persistence in a course of action, especially in spite of difficulties. First Corinthians 9:24 says that we are to "run in such a way as to get the prize."

Not long ago, I was visiting San Francisco, California, on a business trip. While there, I had the opportunity to bike across the Golden Gate Bridge. Believing I was in good shape and mounting my bike with helmet in hand, I soon learned that my bike adventure was a bit more than I had anticipated. With cold temperatures, strong gusty winds, and some very steep hills, the trek across the Golden Gate Bridge was definitely a challenge. What I thought would be an enjoyable scenic bike ride turned into a demanding obstacle course.

Midway across the bridge, I realized that I had not taken my eyes off of the path I was biking on because of the obstacles all around me. I was missing the beautiful view of the bay. I was running the race to finish the course and had not enjoyed the ride for a single moment. With that thought, I stopped in the middle of the bridge, dismounted from my bike, and took in the full view of the bay. As I stood midpoint on the bridge, I breathed in the spectacular view and all of its magnificent beauty. Ah, what a splendid sight. To think about this now, I realize that I nearly lost the prize of taking in God's beautiful creation.

Too often in life, we run the race to finish what we set out to accomplish, forgetting to stop and take in the sights and sounds God has created specifically for us. While God's Word declares we are to run the race with perseverance and in a way to win the race, take a few minutes today to enjoy the views around you. God will help you to the finish line.

Prayer

Father, You are the God of victory who helps me win the race set before me. Give me strength and courage today to run my course with joy and Your glory. Amen.

All God's Children

Main Text

Galatians 3:26–27: "So in Christ Jesus you are all children of God through faith, for all of you who were baptized into Christ have clothed yourselves with Christ."

Meditation

Over the past year, I have taken an interest in learning about my ancestry on both my father's and mother's sides of the family. In particular, I have been studying the history and genealogy of my father. Although I am not a history buff, I have discovered some fascinating information. There are many Internet sites and historical journals that have recorded history, and I did not know where to go, what to look for, and whom to ask. So I did as any good steward would—I asked questions about my ancestry of my dearest and oldest living relatives. Because they have lived the longest, seen the most, and would have the greatest depth of information about my heritage, I knew they would be a great resource.

After several months of discovery, my first real breakthrough occurred. I found a solid lead. How exiting to learn of relatives you did not know about and who didn't know about you. Communication with a stranger in another country makes for an intimidating first encounter. Will you be accepted, questioned, frowned upon, or simply dismissed?

As I worked on my father's ancestry, I was reminded of the scriptures that talk about the fact that we are all sons and daughters of Jesus Christ, and that we have an extended family of brothers and sisters in Jesus all around the world. One Father with many siblings. Imagine that family reunion someday when all the brothers and sisters in Christ will meet for the first time. Although our earthly families are wonderful, our heavenly family of other believers will be together for a celebration that will last an eternity. So much for a weekend family reunion.

Galatians 3:26–27 tells us, "So in Christ Jesus you are all children of God through faith, for all of you who were baptized into Christ have clothed yourselves with Christ." Someday we will get to meet our extended relatives in heaven. What a wonderful thought to know that our heavenly Father will reunite His entire family for eternity in heaven.

Prayer

Father, You are a faithful God. I can be assured of my heavenly home because Your Word declares You are my Father and that You are coming back for me soon. Keep me safe this day and lead me to the places You need me to go. Cause me to be obedient to You. Thank You, Father. Amen.

On Fire but Not Consumed

Main Text

Exodus 3:3: "So Moses thought, 'I will go over and see this strange sight—why the bush does not burn up.'"

Meditation

I am amazed by God's Word. I mean, really amazed by the peculiar stories found in the Bible. I like to think that Hollywood has creative geniuses, but God outshines them all with creativity and imagination.

Imagine you are out in the field tending to your animals when you look up and see an angel standing in the middle of a bush that is on fire. What do you do? Sounds like some kind of riddle, doesn't it? Moses witnessed such an incredible act in Exodus 3. He was tending to his father-in-law's flock when he looked up and saw an angel standing in the middle of a bush that was on fire. Moses could hardly believe his eyes and decided to take a closer look. As he walked toward the bush, he noticed that it was on fire; however, the fire was not consuming it. God saw Moses checking out His burning bush and called out his name, "Moses! Moses!" (v. 4). I am not sure about you, but if I were standing in front of a burning bush and it was calling my name, I don't know how I would react. I love Moses' response to God's call; he said, "Here I am" (v. 4).

Can you picture yourself talking to a burning bush? Seems pretty strange to me. What I have learned is that nothing is strange in God's sight. God sometimes needs to capture our attention. In order to do so, He may use some very unconventional means, like a burning bush. The response that Moses gave God after he heard God calling his name is powerful. Do you think Moses knew what he was about to commit to as he responded to God? When God calls your name from your burning bush, will you to be ready to respond, "Here I am"?

Prayer

Father God, give me the courage to respond to Your call with, "Here I am." Let me be sensitive to Your way and the things You have for me. Amen.

Day 30

Watchman

Main Text

Matthew 25:13: "Therefore keep watch, because you do not know the day or the hour."

Meditation

A *watchman* is an old term that dates back to the mid-1800s when cities and villages would set up guard posts manned with watchmen to alert those in a city or village of approaching danger. Usually watchmen worked at night, when most attacks would take place. In a community, the watchman was the third most unwanted job followed only by the cemetery clerk and mortician.

With terrible hours, poor pay, and potential risk of death, townspeople avoided this position and often shunned the person in this job. A watchman's duties could never be neglected, even for a night. A watchman never knew the date, time, or place that an enemy might attack. He needed to be on guard at every moment, ready to alert the city or village he guarded. It strikes me as odd that such an important job was given to a person who was respected so little by those he guarded. One would think that the best qualified would be placed in this position.

Matthew 25:13 tells us that we do not know the day or the hour that the Son of man will return. He will sneak in like a thief in the night, and those who have accepted Jesus Christ as Savior will be taken away. Gone to heaven. Wow! That sounds like a job for a watchman. Jesus Christ told us to be on guard. Christ clearly warned us that we must be ready at any given moment.

Just like the watchman, we must be prepared. There will be no one to give us a warning. Instead, in an instant we will be taken to be with the Father. The overriding question is, are you ready? Have you given your heart to Jesus and are you watching for His return? Jesus asks that we be watchmen standing guard for His return.

Prayer

Jesus, I ask that You guard my heart today. Protect, guide, and lead me this day. Let me be ready at all times, seeking You and desiring to do Your will. Thank You for Your protection and grace. Keep me safe this day. Amen.

Careful What You Say

Main Text

Matthew 12:36–37: "But I tell you that everyone will have to give account on the day of judgment for every empty word they have spoken. For by your words you will be acquitted, and by your words you will be condemned."

Meditation

Have you ever thought about your tongue? The tongue has eight muscles that allow for great movement and the ability to taste, swallow, and speak. There are many sayings that relate to the tongue: "I have something on the tip of my tongue," "bite your tongue," or how about "tongue and cheek." The average person can speak 175 words per minute. The tongue is a powerful tool. We can build up or tear down with our words. The tone we use can provide comfort or grief. The attitude in which we speak can reaffirm or destroy. With eight muscles, we have the ability to cause irreversible damage, break a friendship, drive a wedge between family members and friends, or create distrust. The tongue can also build one another up. The words we speak can praise someone, light spirits, engage, support, minister, and affirm.

Matthew's gospel is a powerful book demonstrating God's call to repentance and grace in Jesus Christ. "I tell you that everyone will have to give account on the day of judgment for every empty word they have spoken. For by your words you will be acquitted, and by your words you will be condemned" (12:36–37). Matthew clearly tells us that we will be judged for what we have said when Jesus Christ returns. We will either be blessed and praised or condemned and rebuked for our words.

Will you practice control of your tongue today so that the words you say will bring glory to the Father up above?

Prayer

Father, help me control my tongue and use words that will be worthy and acceptable to You. Cause me to understand that the words I say impact others. Jesus, let me be an encourager in You. Amen.

Sweet Aroma

Main Text

2 Corinthians 2:15: "For we are to God the pleasing aroma of Christ among those who are being saved and those who are perishing."

Meditation

Have you ever entered a room where the aroma of freshly baked cookies or the sweet fragrance of your favorite food filled the air? Recently, while on vacation, I took a tour of a chocolate factory. Not just any chocolate factory, but one of the finest chocolate factories in the United States. I was impressed to learn that chocolate is classified as a fruit. That's right, a fruit. Sounds too good to be true, doesn't it? Cocoa seeds, as they are commonly called, are grown in shells on trees that look similar to those on plum trees. These shells are all handpicked at just the perfect ripe stage and turned into wonderful sweet chocolate.

As I was making my way through the chocolate factory, I was greeted with the sugary fragrance of chocolate. The air seemed to come alive with the sweet flavor of the chocolate and caused a yearning in me to want chocolate. Anticipating our cravings, our tour guide made sure our sweet tooth was satisfied by providing an endless supply of all kinds of chocolate samples.

Walking into the processing area and taking in the fragrant smells of chocolate, I could not help but be reminded of the Scripture verse that talks about this: "We are to God the pleasing aroma of Christ" (2 Corinthians 2:15). The beauty and fresh aroma of Jesus in our lives has the power to meet our every want and desire. The Word of God clearly states Jesus is our sweet Savior and is always there to meet us where we are, regardless of what life challenges we may be facing. We need to trust Him and rely on Him to satisfy our "sweet tooth" by basking in His sweet, beautiful glory.

The next time you bite into a piece of chocolate, thank Jesus for being your sweet Savior, the one who satisfies.

Prayer

God, You are my sweet Savior, meeting my ever need. I ask that You cause me to be reminded of Your sweet fragrance and to share it with those I come in contact with today. Amen.

Day 33

It Taste Like Chicken

Main Text

Matthew 3:4: "John's clothes were made of camel's hair, and he had a leather belt around his waist. His food was locusts and wild honey."

Meditation

Do you have a favorite food? Mine is chicken. Anything chicken. Chicken and dumpling soup, chicken nuggets, grilled chicken, fried chicken, and chicken-topped pizza, to name just a few. I think you get the picture. My wife tells me I am difficult to cook for because I only want chicken. I think I am easy to cook for because I only want chicken.

John the Baptist was a prophet who was sent to prepare the way for the coming of the Messiah. By nature, John the Baptist was a fiery, plain, no-frills type of guy. Matthew records that John the Baptist's clothes were made of camel hair, and he wore a leather belt around his waist. Nothing wrong with that, right? Simple, straightforward. Unlike Jesus, John the Baptist did not go from place to place to preach, but instead remained in one spot. John the Baptist developed a large following of disciples and made his "headquarters," as it were, in a cave on the east side of the Jordon River. And—are you ready for this?— John's diet consisted of mainly locust and honey. That's right, locust and honey. Chicken is looking pretty good about now, isn't it?

A guy who had a powerful ministry for Jesus Christ and made an impact in spreading the gospel, and his primary diet was a plate of grasshoppers. I tease my wife that grasshoppers maybe taste like chicken, and if John the Baptist could survive on grasshoppers, I can survive on chicken.

The real element to focus on isn't what John the Baptist ate, but what he did to serve God. John the Baptist, in his simple life, dress, and diet, impacted many for the kingdom of God. When God chooses people, He looks at the heart, not at what they wear, eat, drive, or live in. I challenge you to focus on the things in your life that will influence the kingdom of Christ. What can you do to touch others and lead them to the saving knowledge of Jesus? Take an inventory of your life, and use the talents and skills God has blessed you with to encouragement others in Jesus' name.

Prayer

Jesus, thank You for working in my life. Cause me to take the plain and simple and turn it into a "Jesus" moment that will inspire others to seek You. Amen.

Day 34

All God's Creatures

Main Text

Genesis 1:25: "God made the wild animals according to their kinds, the livestock according to their kinds, and all the creatures that move along the ground according to their kinds. And God saw that it was good."

Meditation

What is the craziest-looking animal you've ever seen? Recently, I saw a website of the weirdest-looking animals on the planet. Number one on the list was the Emperor tamarin (from the monkey species) followed by the white-faced saki monkey. Both animals are quite fun to look at with their intriguing, unique features.

As I scrolled through the webpage of the weirdest-looking animals on the planet, I could not help but chuckle at the uniqueness and individuality of each animal. Although some of the animals were strange looking, God made them all. While I was looking at the photos, I could not help but smile that God has an awesome sense of humor. To think that God single-handedly created every animal on days five and six of creation and let Adam give each of them name. What a humbling thought to know that God cared enough for each animal to give it special characteristics and traits that were distinctive.

Genesis records the creation of God's handiwork. Genesis 1:25 says, "God made the wild animals according to their kinds." I love in particular the last sentence of this verse: "And God saw that it was good." I can only imagine what God thought as He was creating animals. Do you think He laughed to Himself? Was He trying to show us His majesty through creation? One thing I am sure of is that God is the master Creator.

God certainly cares about His creation. He cares about each animal, each bird, and each wild beast that roams the earth. If He cares for each animal in a special way, how much more does He care for you? God created all things including you, with your unique design, with your own personality and DNA. As you ponder creation by God, thank Him for making every living thing for His purpose and glory. Thank Him for making you uniquely you.

Prayer

God, You are Creator of all. You crafted and designed the earth and all things on it. Thank You for giving me Your creation to appreciate, and thank You for making me who I am. Amen.

How Far Is Heaven?

Main Text

Nehemiah 9:6: "You alone are the LORD. You made the heavens, even the highest heavens, and all their starry host, the earth and all that is on it, the seas and all that is in them. You give life to everything, and the multitudes of heaven worship you."

Meditation

Have you ever stopped to consider that the sun is 91 million miles from earth at its closest point and 95 million miles from earth at its farthest distance? Because the earth does not travel around the sun in a perfect circle, but instead in an elliptical orbit, the distance from the earth to the sun changes during the year. Think about the marvel of how the universe was created. The sun, moon, planets, stars, galaxies, air, wind . . . the list is endless. All these things created by God are at the command of His voice.

I am fascinated when NASA launches a shuttle. I wait with eager anticipation to learn of the new mystery or discoveries that will be made. Consider the details of the universe, how vast and how wide God created the heavens and the earth. Imagine the science project your kid could create if we knew the mysteries of the unknown universe.

Nehemiah 9:6 states, "You alone are the LORD. You made the heavens, even the highest heavens, and all their starry host." Someday when I get to heaven I'm going to ask God to tell me all about the mysteries of the heavens. I'd really like to know how far earth is from heaven. Until we reach our heavenly home, I can only dream about the mysteries God has created.

Prayer

Your Word declares You created the heavens and the earth and all that is on them. What a marvelous creation. Thank You, Father, for Your awesome creation. Bless this day that You have made specifically for me. Amen.

Victory

Main Text

1 Corinthians 15:57: "But thanks be to God! He gives us the victory through our Lord Jesus Christ."

Meditation

Have you ever wanted to be an Olympic athlete? Like many people, I love watching the Olympics on television. The pomp and circumstance of the opening ceremony, the athletes dressed in their native costumes, and the proud look on each athlete's face as the camera pans by . . . it all looks so fun and easy.

If you ever have the opportunity to visit the Olympics, or even an Olympic Village where the games were held in the past, I recommend you go. On a recent vacation, I went to an Olympic village and I imagined myself as an Olympic athlete. I could hear the roar of the crowd, the cheering of the fans, the announcement of my name, and most important, I could see myself standing as a final medalist on the winner's podium. It's only a dream, but it's all mine.

Too often we think that the physical condition of an athlete is most important in winning. Recently, I read an article on the mental conditioning of Olympic athletes. Although they train their physical bodies, they also train their minds. Olympic athletes go through a mental conditioning where they envision themselves winning their race. They rehearse in their minds over and over the steps, movements, jumps, kicks, throws, and exact timing of their event.

You see, we can condition our bodies, but equally as important is conditioning our minds. The Bible talks about conditioning our minds and keeping our minds on the things above, not on things on the earth. What we read, what we see, and what we take in impacts our minds. We need to focus on Jesus Christ and the things He sets before us.

As I stood on my "pretend" winner's platform, I relished in my gold-medal placement. My dream brought an earthy victory to mind, but Jesus brings sweet victory to our lives when we trust in Him. Are you conditioning your mind with the things of Jesus Christ? Are you focusing on events that will bring honor to Jesus? If not, ask Jesus to give you clear direction.

Prayer

Father, let me daily seek after the things that keep my mind and heart in tune with You. Bring victory to my life through Your grace and goodness. Let me be an overcomer in all things as I stay focused on the things above. Grant Your mercy to me now, I pray. Amen.

Take Up Your Mat

Main Text

Mark 2:11–12: "'I tell you, get up, take your mat and go home.' He got up, took his mat and walked out in full view of them all. This amazed everyone and they praised God, saying, 'We have never seen anything like this!'"

Meditation

You hear about the health struggles of the world in nearly every newscast, you read about them in the daily newspaper, and they bombard you over the radio. People are ill, the cost of health care has skyrocketed, and masses of people are uninsured. If you are like me, sometimes hearing all of these things is just too much to take in. We know costs are high and people are ill, but what is the solution to the issues?

As I listened to the morning news, I was reminded of the lame man whose friends lowered him through the top story of a building to place him in front of Jesus (Mark 2:1–12). The crowd was massive because so many wanted to hear Jesus or to simply get a glimpse of Him or to touch Him in hopes of being healed by the Master. I can see the scene in my mind. The lame man summoned four of his friends to help him get to Jesus. As they surveyed the situation, they saw no way of getting close to Jesus. Then one of them came up with a plan. Perhaps a crazy plan, but a plan nonetheless. I can hear the conversation: "Come on, guys, we can do this. All we have to do is get to the roof, cut a hole in it, and lower him down right in front of Jesus. What's the worst that could happen?"

The details unfolded just as they had strategically planned. They got to the roof, the hole was cut, and the lame man was lowered with precision right in front of Jesus. Imagine the look on Jesus' face as He saw this guy coming down from the ceiling. What do you think was going through the lame man's mind as he approached Jesus? All this was occurring in front of a crowd of witnesses and there was no turning back. When Jesus saw the faith of the man's friends, He said, "I tell you, get up, take your mat and go home" (v. 11).

Incredible, isn't it? Plans made, plans carried out, and a man was healed by Jesus Christ, the divine Healer. Regardless of who we are, what we do, where we live, or the circumstance we are in, Jesus can heal. Jesus can make you completely whole. Ask Him today for what you need.

Prayer

Jesus, You are the divine Healer who can make me whole in an instant. Give me faith to trust You to heal and restore. Thank You, Jesus. Amen.

Day 38

It's a Heart Thing

Main Text

Matthew 5:8: "Blessed are the pure in heart, for they will see God."

Meditation

Your heart will beat on average 100,000 times per day, or in a lifetime, 2.5 billion times. Your heart circulates the six quarts of blood found in your body an average of three times per minute. The heart is an amazing muscular organ that is responsible for keeping you alive by pumping blood through your body.

In Matthew 5:8, Jesus calls us to be pure of heart. What does this mean? The Greek word for *pure* is *katharos*. It means to be "clean, blameless, and unstained from guilt." Being pure in heart is having a personal relationship with Jesus Christ. A pure heart has no malice, envy, deceit, or hidden motives, but rather has an outward attitude of openness and a desire to serve and please Jesus. The only way to have a pure heart is to ask Jesus Christ to cleanse you and make you new through His forgiving grace. There are no other options that can give you a pure, forgiven heart. You may try living a good life by doing good works, helping and serving others, and giving to those in need, all of which are wonderful things. But all of these attempts to have a pure heart will fail. Scripture is clear that in order to have a personal relationship with Jesus Christ, you must ask Jesus to change your heart. Jesus desires to provide you with a clean, blameless heart free from guilt and sin. Have you sought a pure heart? If not, reach out to Jesus today and ask for a heart-changing transformation. It's a heart thing only He can deliver.

Prayer

How awesome You are, Father, that You give life to my body and soul. Guard my heart today as I strive to be blameless in You. Thank You, Jesus, for creating in me a clean heart. Amen.

We All Make Mistakes

Main Text

John 3:16: "For God so loved the world that he gave his one and only Son, that whoever believeth in him shall not perish but have eternal life."

Meditation

I am not ashamed to admit that I make mistakes. We all do. When I make mistakes, I often feel upset with myself and question my judgment as I try to reconcile why I did what I did.

Mistakes come in all shapes and sizes and are no respecter of persons. The simple Bible verse that we learned as children from John 3:16 clearly tells us that we have forgiveness and peace in Jesus when we ask for forgiveness. John 3:16 is a profound scripture that delivers redemption to us regardless of what we have said or done. If we ask to be forgiven and believe that Jesus has paid the ultimate price for our mistakes, He is just and forgives us. From a human perspective, mistakes happen. How we respond to the mistakes we've made impacts the growth of our character. It is hard to admit to mistakes. Most of us never set out to intentionally sin or hurt someone. The quality of our character, however, is measured by how we respond. We are called to pray daily that Jesus will help us develop the character He desires to nurture in us.

God so loved the world. He gave His one and only Son for you and me so that if we will only believe in Him, He will give us eternal life. Ponder this scripture today in your heart and know that God's love is all sufficient to redeem you from the mistakes you have made. Isn't it wonderful to know that we have a heavenly Father who knows who we are and loves us for who we are, even when we make mistakes that make us feel inadequate to receive God's love?

Prayer

Jesus, You love me so much that You gave Your life so that I might be set free. Help me live a life filled with Your grace that I may make an impact for You. Amen.

Day 40

What's in Your Hand?

Main Text

Exodus 7:10: "So Moses and Aaron went to Pharaoh and did just as the LORD commanded. Aaron threw his staff down in front of Pharaoh and his officials, and it became a snake."

Meditation

Many little boys dream of being a fireman and lots of little girls dream of being a princess. Remember when you dreamed about what you'd be when you grew up? We had dreams about our future. Some of us dreamed of being a doctor, a veterinarian, a famous singer, a dancer, or a farmer. Whatever your dream, God gives each of us gifts and talents to use for Him.

The desires God places in our hearts are real, and He asks that we be diligent in whatever He places in our hands as life's work. As Aaron and Moses were about to stand before Pharaoh, God instructed them to use what was in their hands as a sign of God's power in their life. Exodus 7:10 tells us, "So Moses and Aaron went to Pharaoh and did just as the LORD commanded. Aaron threw his staff down in front of Pharaoh and his officials, and it became a snake."

I believe the symbolism of the staff in Aaron's hands was God's way of using what Aaron was comfortable with. A simple staff, a walking stick, was common in biblical days and something that Aaron used daily. A staff or a rod was often representative of power or authority. As I dwell on this scripture, I see God taking the simple piece of wood that He had placed in Aaron's hand and turning it into a snake, something not possible by human hands but possible by the hand of God. You see, I believe God demonstrated His power through ordinary means that Aaron was comfortable with to make a profound statement in front of Pharaoh.

What has God placed in your hand that He wants to use for His purpose? If God gives you the talent to sing, then sing. If He bestowed you with the ability to build, then build. Did He give you the ability to teach? Then teach. Whatever tool or item God has placed in your hand, be obedient in using it for His glory. When we are willing to use what God has given us, I believe He will make things come alive before our very eyes just as He did with Aaron and his staff. What an awesome opportunity we have to see God use what is in our hands. Are you willing to use the gifts and talents God has given you for His kingdom?

Prayer

Father, I pray that You take what is in my hands and bring it to life. Cause me to use my talent and skill that You have given me to impact those around me. I know that when I trust You, I can be assured of glorious victory in Your name. Amen.

Oh, How Sweet

Main Text

Psalm 119:103: "How sweet are your words to my taste, sweeter than honey to my mouth!"

Meditation

Americans, including me, have an obsession with sweets, in particular chocolate. In 1894, history was made when Milton Hersey developed the rich-tasting flavor of his chocolate and began producing it as a coating for his caramels. As they say, "and the rest is history." Today, the average American consumes eleven pounds of chocolate on an annual basis, and I certainly do my part in keeping the average American chocolate consumption at eleven pounds per year.

Regardless of how you enjoy your chocolate, it pleases your palette and satisfies your cravings for something sweet. Psalm 119, with 176 verses, is the longest chapter in the Bible and is believed to have been written by David. David penned his thoughts on how sweet and all sufficient the Word of God is. In verse 103, he said the Word of God is "sweeter than honey to my mouth!"

The Word of God is truly sweet, powerful, all sufficient, and life changing. It creates a yearning in us to read His Word more often and to learn of Jesus more each day. The Word of God is like a chocolate obsession—the more you read, the more you crave it. Are you getting your daily allowance of God's Word by reading and studying the Bible? If not, start today. I can promise you that it satisfies.

Prayer

Jesus, thank You for Your Word that is sweeter than honey and brings peace and grace to my life. Give me understanding and a desire to study Your Word daily. Amen.

Who Is Speaking?

Main Text

Genesis 11:9: "That is why it was called Babel—because there the LORD confused the language of the whole world. From there the LORD scattered them over the face of the whole earth."

Meditation

Recently I was giving a presentation to a group containing a lot of immigrants who could speak multiple languages. I am always intrigued by individuals who can fluently speak multiple languages since I cannot. As we broke for lunch that day, I paid particular attention to how individuals grouped themselves according to their country of origin. Over lunch, I was able to identify several languages coming from all areas of the dining room. Although it was confusing to me because I did not speak any of the languages, each table group carried on a seamless conversation, laughed, and enjoyed each other's company.

Driving home, I replayed that time over and over again. As I thought about the activity of the day, it reminded me of the Bible story of the Tower of Babel in Genesis 11 where God reached down and touched the tongue of each individual and caused them to suddenly begin to speak a different language. Verse 8 says that the "LORD confused the language of the whole world." God changed the direction of mankind in a single act by crafting all languages of the world. What an astounding act by our Creator.

Those of us who do not speak more than one language may not understand others who speak a different language, but we can take delight in knowing that God has created all mankind and their languages for His glory. The next time you find yourself in a situation where you cannot understand the language or culture of others, recognize that God Himself is the Creator of all things and appreciate the fact that God is perfect in all things.

Prayer

Father, thank You for creating beautiful languages that bring people around the world together to worship You. I ask that You craft the language of Jesus Christ on my heart to love others as You love me. Amen.

Day 43

Angels

Main Text

Daniel 6:22: "My God sent his angel, and he shut the mouths of the lions. They have not hurt me, because I was found innocent in his sight. Nor have I ever done any wrong before you, Your Majesty."

Meditation

We see images of angels in art and movies, but have you ever wondered what the Bible has to say about angels? Reflect for a moment on the number of occurrences you can name in the Bible where an angel appeared. Angels announced the birth of Jesus, and a group of angels appeared at the tomb of Jesus where they declared to Mary and Maratha that He was alive. Then there was the angel Gabriel that appeared to Mary to tell her she would have a son. One of my favorite angel appearances is when an angel closed the mouths of the lions in the story of Daniel in the lions' den. And of course you probably remember the angel that appeared in the fiery furnace to keep Shadrach, Meshach, and Abednego safe.

Whatever your memory of angels from Scripture, we know that God planned these appearances for a specific reason. Scripture does not tell us many specifics about angels. What we do know is that angels are ministering spirits and do not have physical bodies, although we know angels have appeared in body form. Angels have been created by God to serve Him in a variety of ways. In Scripture, we find angels worshiping and praising God, acting as messengers, and guiding people as they did for Joseph at the birth of Jesus. Angels have provided, protected, delivered, encouraged, strengthened, been used by God to answer prayers, and even cared for people at the time of death.

Angels are all around us and were created by God to assist Him in His reign. Angels have a great responsibility and are often sent to help us. As you go through your day today, keep the promise of God's Word in your heart that His angels go about leading and helping us on God's command. Isn't it awesome that we serve a God who gives His angels charge over us?

Prayer

God, You are powerful and all-knowing, and I am so grateful that You have sent Your angels to help me in my time of need. Let me seek You and Your will for my life. Send Your angels even now on my behalf. Amen.

Day 44

Crazy Birds

Main Text

I Kings 17:6: "The ravens brought him bread and meat in the morning and bread and meat in the evening, and he drank from the brook."

Meditation

I have a group of birds that have taken over my yard and made it their priority in life to harm me. As crazy as it sounds, I believe this wild posse of birds has devised a plan to attack me each time I mow the lawn. The wildest event takes place each time I take the lawn mower out of the garage. I will be minding my own business mowing the lawn when out of nowhere, this bird gang begins to swarm the lawn mower, weaving in and out, swooping down in an attack formation directly at my head. No matter what I do, I cannot disarm this bandit group of birds. I have no idea what I have done to these birds to provoke such aggressive behavior. I am convinced that it is only a matter of time before they catch me off guard and do me in.

I am reminded of another, not-so-aggressive set of birds that God used to feed His prophet Elijah. Elijah delivered some bad news to King Ahab. Because of his wickedness, there would be no rain for several years in his kingdom. This angered the king greatly, that a prophet of God would predict such an event. God sent word to Elijah that he should flee from the king's presence and hide in the Kerith Ravine, where he would be safe from the king's vengeance.

Elijah obeyed God and made his way to the ravine. God also told Elijah that He would provide food and water for him daily. Are you ready for this? God provided food and water to Elijah by sending ravens in both the morning and the evening. Imagine a group of birds serving you breakfast and dinner daily. As I think about this, I am amazed at the methods God uses to take care of His children. Sometimes God's delivery methods are a bit unusual; however, they serve the intended purpose.

The next time you see a group of birds crisscrossing in the sky, contemplate the story of Elijah and the ravens that fed him. Remember that God uses unusual means to carry out His work, even birds of the air.

Prayer

Father, You are the God that commands even the birds of the air on my behalf. Thank You for providing exactly what I need. Amen.

Strong Man

Main Text

Isaiah 40:31: "But those who hope in the LORD will renew their strength. They will soar on wings like eagles; they will run and not grow weary, they will walk and not be faint."

Meditation

The word *strength* can solicit many meanings. We recognize strength in terms of character, leadership, and attitude. Most often, however, we think of strength in terms of physical potential. How many pounds can someone deadlift, arm curl, bench press, or leg press? One wildly strange physical test of strength is how many pounds you can lift using only your tongue. That's right, only your tongue. As odd as it may sound, the Genius Book of World Records identifies that on August 1, 2008, a man deadlifted just a little over twenty-seven pounds of weight using only his tongue.

I am not sure I would ever want to be the world record holder for a tongue deadlift. I do know that Jesus Christ has promised to give me strength when I need it. Isaiah 40:31 says, "But those who hope in the LORD will renew their strength. They will soar on wings like eagles." What a glorious assurance that when we need help we have hope in Jesus Christ and can be confident that He will renew our strength. Daily we are challenged by the pressures of life, children, work, church, finances, and school. Whatever may cause your state of weariness, know that you can be strengthened by God.

The next time you need strength to carry on, look to Jesus. He has promised to help.

Prayer

Father, You are my daily strength. Thank You for being there for me each day. Let me run this day and not grow weary. In Your powerful name, Amen.

Day 46

Cruising Altitude

Main Text

John: 14:6: "Jesus answered, 'I am the way and the truth and the life. No one comes to the Father except through me.'"

Meditation

"We have reached our cruising altitude of thirty-eight thousand feet, and you can now use your approved electronic devices." Those of you who have flown have no doubt heard a similar announcement. As I sat in my seat taking in those words, I began to think about the fact that I was hovering above the ground at thirty-eight thousand feet at a speed of 530 mph.

Too often in life, we hear things that seem to cause disbelief. There is an old cliché that says, "If something sounds too good to be true, it probably is." Daily we are told what to believe, when to believe, and why to believe; however, often we do not validate the information but instead take the information for what is stated. I wonder how many things we believe about life that are not accurate but instead are embellished or have the truth stretched.

One thing I am sure of is the fact that God and His word are true. It says in John 14:6 that Jesus is "the way, the truth, and the life." The Bible clearly identifies Jesus Christ as the one truth for all people. We need to take that truth and apply it to our daily lives. When we see things around us that may sound unbelievable, we can be assured that there is an all-knowing and all-trusting God who leads and directs us throughout each day.

As you move through your day and encounter things that seem to be unbelievable, stop and question their validity. In the meantime, you can be confident that God has His hand on you. Give Him thanks today, for He is good and His truth is everlasting. Share with someone God's divine truth that has set you free; it might just change that person's life.

Prayer

Jesus, Your Word is truth and guides me as I trust in You. Cause me to be lifted up in You this day and every day, knowing Your hand is upon me. I love You, Father, and thank You for Your goodness and truth. Amen.

Day 47

I Shall Not Be Moved

Main Text

Psalm 62:6: "Truly he is my rock and my salvation; he is my fortress, I will not be shaken."

Meditation

The German Alps is part of a mountain range that touches eight countries and spans 750 miles. The Alps are also known as the Bavarian Alps because they intersect with the borders of Switzerland, Italy, and Austria. This massive mountain region is spectacular and draws visitors from around the world. According to Wikipedia, the average year-round temperature at the top is -4.8 Celsius.

While on vacation in Germany, I had the opportunity to travel up the side of the Alps in a cable car. At first I was a bit reluctant to board the cable car that would make its way up the side of mountain. Standing on the ground looking upward at the mountain is a captivating view that does not do justice to the Alps' reputation. With a bit of encouragement from those around me, I boarded the cable car, which by the way is held in midair by four small cables; I will confess I was nervous.

The ascent up the side of the mountain was spectacular, actually breathtaking; so much so that I failed to recognize until I was near the top of the mountain that the little cable car (in comparison to the massive Alps) had made its way flawlessly to the top. Thankful for a safe journey, I exited the cable car and made my way to the observation deck for a closer look at the magnificent view. On a clear day, you can see the Alps in all the adjoining countries, which provides an indescribable scene. As I stood atop of the German-sided Alps, the old hymn "I Shall

Not Be, I Shall Not Be Moved" captured my mind. I was breathless from the beauty God had created. I prayed and thanked God for His awe-inspiring creation and was humbled to be able to stand there in that moment and take in His glory.

God's Word proclaims He is the Rock that cannot be moved. I have no idea what God was thinking when He created the Alps. But I am confident that God created the gigantic landscape with a spectacular view. If God is for us, who can be against us?

Prayer

God, You have created a magnificent world for me to enjoy. May I know and recognize You as the Rock of my salvation. Let me understand and know Your vastness and beauty. Bless me this day. In Your faithful name I pray. Amen.

Day 48

Lights, Camera, Action

Main Text

2 Timothy 3:16–17: "All Scripture is God-breathed and is useful for teaching, rebuking, correcting and training in righteousness, so that the servant of God may be thoroughly equipped for every good work."

Meditation

I have had the opportunity to host a public access television show in my local community for several years. The experience has been very enjoyable and has allowed me to meet many new people who are doing wonderful things to enhance the municipal they live and work in. I have had the pleasure of interviewing local celebrities, government officials, and guests who are local heroes.

I like to think of the Bible as a stage where stories can come to life. The Bible is filled with so many wonderful and powerful stories that change the way we live, think, and interact with one another. The Bible is God's inspired Word for His people. Imagine for a moment that you had a talk show and could invite the characters from the Bible. What would you ask your favorite Bible character? I know I would have a list of questions to ask Mary, the mother of Jesus. What kind of child was Jesus? Did He eat His peas and drink His milk? What would you talk to Gabriel, the archangel, about? Think about what Gabriel got to see and do. I want to hear more. Can you imagine the interview with David? I would not know where to start my questions. From a shepherd boy to a giant slayer to king. All of these characters and more in the Bible are fascinating to me. The Word of God gives us so much to read and take in, yet there are so many more questions and details I want to know that were not provided in the Bible.

Read God's Word and let it soak deep into your mind and heart. In 2 Timothy 3:16–17, we read that "all Scripture is God-breathed and is useful for teaching, rebuking, correcting, and training in righteousness, so that the servant of God may be thoroughly equipped for every good work." We know that the Bible is the account of God's action in the world and His purpose for all creation. Writing the Bible took over sixteen centuries and is the work of over forty authors. It is quite an amazing collection of sixty-six books, all containing the message God desired to give to us. Read His Word and cherish it deep in your heart. You will be glad you did.

Prayer

God, Your Word is life to my soul. Let me read and study Your Word with an open, clear mind that I might receive what You have for me. Amen.

The Glory of the Lord

Main Text

Psalm 19:1: "The heavens declare the glory of God; and the skies proclaim the work of his hands."

Meditation

My wife was gone a few weekends ago visiting family and friends, so I decided to do one of my favorite things: take a sunrise bicycle ride. There is nothing like it. The early-morning air, the dew still on the grass, the birds singing their morning songs. As I began my ride at a very early hour, I started to worship God and give Him praise for all the marvelous things He has done and what He has created. As I praised Him, I noticed just over the horizon in front of me the breaking of the sunrise. I stopped for a few minutes on my morning trek to take in the glorious view and ponder the workmanship of our Creator. How awesome is it that God created these views for me? The verse in Psalm 19 came to mind: "The heavens declare the glory of God." Often we are too busy to notice the workmanship of God. We are caught up in our daily routines and the hustle and bustle of life that we do not stop for even a moment and take in what God has created. You see, God created the heavens and the earth and specifically gave them to us to enjoy.

When was the last time that you took a few minutes to stop or even slow down to take in the handiwork of God? If you are like me, not often enough. Take some time this week to look around you. I promise you will find God's handiwork all around. Thank Him for His beautiful design that He provided to us, and like the chief musician David, you too will be able to declare the glory of God.

Prayer

God, You have made the heavens and the earth for my enjoyment and refreshing. Cause me to take note of the things You have given me, and let me rejoice in knowing You as the Creator of all things. Amen.

Day 50

For the Sake of the Call

Main Text

Romans 10:15: "And how can anyone preach unless they are sent? As it is written: 'How beautiful are the feet of those who bring good news!'"

Meditation

I have a friend who has been a missionary for over thirty years, serving Christ in a foreign country halfway around the world. He and his wife have left family, friends, and all of the things you and I know as part of normal life to serve Christ as missionaries. Many times during the month, the electricity is cut, the phone doesn't work, gas is not available for the car, and the list goes on. Many of the things you and I take for granted are not available to my missionary friends. Think about how giving up your conveniences would change your world. When I asked them why they chose to become missionaries, they responded, "If we didn't go, who would have?"

As I think about that statement, "If we didn't go, who would have?" it burns in my soul. All too often we expect others to go and to give, but what if God was calling you? Could you abandon all for the cause of Christ and move to a foreign county with your family and serve Christ? Would you be willing to cash it all in and live life with daily uncertainties? If you are honest with yourself, you may have significant reservation about answering the call.

Romans 10:15 says, "And how can anyone preach unless they are sent?" I believe there is a special calling on the lives of missionaries. They give up so much for the sake of presenting the gospel so that others all around the world may come to know Jesus Christ. It is estimated that over 40 percent of the world's people groups have not yet heard the good news of Jesus. This is a staggering statistic to think that so much of our world has yet to experience the saving knowledge of Jesus. Pray with me that God continues to call people to help reach the world. Perhaps God is calling you. Are you willing to answer His call?

Prayer

Father, instill in me the desire to help reach those who have not heard about You. Open doors and provide opportunities that I might go and preach Your Word to a hurting world. Amen.

Day 51

God Made Us All Different

Main Text

Psalm 139:14: "I praise you because I am fearfully and wonderfully made; your works are wonderful, I know that full well."

Meditation

I love to watch people, no matter where I go or what I am doing. Watching people is fascinating and oftentimes quite humorous. Today I boarded a plane to the West Coast for a meeting. As I sat is my assigned seat, I took the opportunity to do a little people watching as the passengers began to flood onto the plane.

As I carefully watched, I saw sad faces, happy faces, hurting faces, old and wrinkled faces, baby faces, and even a set of faces that looked alike (twins, I presumed). I marveled at the idea that no two people were identical, even the twins. I know God created us each to be distinct, but when you take time to think about this concept, it brings on a whole new meaning. What a marvelous thing that God could create an entire human race and never repeated a single individual. We are all different in looks, personalities, skills, abilities, and attitudes. I am reminded of Psalm 139:14, where God's Word talks about each of us being wonderfully made in the image of God. What an awesome thing to know that there is no one in the world like us. We are perfectly made and a one of a kind.

I am convinced that God has a sense of humor, which is evidenced by His creation of mankind. I think He knew that one of each of us is all that the world could handle. When you have a little time on your hands, do some people watching. You will be amazed at the originality of what God has created. Know that you are loved and have been created by God's hand.

Prayer

God, You are the Creator of all things and I praise You for making me who I am. I know You have made me unique. Father, create in me the fullness of who I need to be for You. Use me today, and help me represent You in all I do. Amen.

Are You Talking to Me?

Main Text

Numbers 22:28: "Then the LORD opened the donkey's mouth, and it said to Balaam, 'What have I done to you to make you beat me these three times?'"

Meditation

Do you remember the old television classic from the early 1960s called *Mr. Ed*? Mr. Ed was a talking horse that was always up to something mischievous. The talking horse was conniving and always looking to pass blame to his owner. The show was timeless and entertaining because we all knew a horse couldn't talk. Scriptures recounts the story of a talking donkey, and it's entertaining too as we see how God used one of His creatures to reach a stubborn man.

A man named Balaam was a sorcerer commissioned by King Balak to curse the Israelites. King Balak despised the Israelites and would stop at nothing to harm them. He promised Balaam that if he would curse the Israelites, he would be generously paid. Balaam took King Balak up on his offer. But God had a different plan for Balaam, and Balaam had no idea that God was about to intervene and protect the Israelites.

Balaam began his journey to complete the task that was assigned to him by the king. In Bible times, the common form of travel was either by foot or on a donkey. Balaam rode a donkey. Balaam mounted his donkey and set out toward the Israelites' camp, when suddenly an angel appeared in the road with a sword. Balaam couldn't see the angel, but it frightened the donkey greatly and caused it to veer off the road into the countryside. Balaam, upset by the donkey's action, beat the donkey to get him back on the road. The angel suddenly appeared for a second time, frightening the donkey again. This time the donkey crushed Balaam's foot against a wall. Balaam again beat the donkey. Surprisingly, the angel appeared to Balaam and the donkey a third time. Immediately, the donkey lay down with Balaam underneath the him. Furious, Balaam beat the donkey with his staff for a third time.

Having had enough of Balaam's action, the Lord opened the donkey's mouth and caused the donkey to speak. As you can imagine, Balaam was stunned to hear his donkey talk. Clearly, the Lord's hand was intervening in Balaam's attempt to harm the Israelites. In order to capture Balaam's attention, God used the unusual means of causing a donkey to speak.

Sometimes we are too stubborn to see what God would have us do and we ignore the obvious signs and direction God sets before us. In times like this, God uses alternative means to get our attention and deliver a message. I'm not sure about you, but I am pretty sure a talking donkey would get my attention just as it did Balaam's. I challenge you to listen for the voice of your talking donkey. What has God been trying to say to you that you have not been willing to hear? Open your mind and your heart and let God capture your ears.

Prayer

God, I pray that You use the unusual to capture my attention and cause me to listen to You. Work in my life that I might be a willing vessel to share Your good news with others. Amen.

Day 53

Sailing the Seas

Main Text

Exodus 14:15–16: "Then the LORD said to Moses, 'Why are you crying out to me? Tell the Israelites to move on. Raise your staff and stretch out your hand over the sea to divide the water so that the Israelites can go through the sea on dry ground.'"

Meditation

Picture this movie scene: You are being chased by a group of angry military men who have pledged to kill you for the beliefs and the moral standards you hold. At any cost they are determined to capture and destroy you and your family. You are being chased across the country, and you come to an impasse. Your back is against the sea, and you are facing your enemy eye to eye. You know the odds are against you and you have two options: fight or flee. Your general stands before you and declares that victory will be yours if you follow his instructions. All odds are against you, and your general tells you to trust his instructions and you will live. What do you do?

Pharaoh was hunting the Israelites and Moses and had chased them to the shoreline of the Red Sea. There was no way of escape, nowhere to run. Moses presented himself before God and cried out to Him asking for help. I so appreciate God's response to Moses' plea: "Why are you crying out to me? Tell the Israelites to move on" (Exodus 14:15). And then He said, "Raise your staff and stretch out your hand over the sea to divide the water" (v. 16). The Word of God tells us that Moses raised his staff over the sea and immediately the sea parted and the Israelites walked through on dry ground. Incredible, wouldn't you say?

Talk about asking and receiving. The miraculous occurred. I believe God's people walked through the Red Sea unharmed, dry, confused, afraid, and awestruck by God's provision. Are you looking for an awestruck God moment in your life? Do you need to walk through your Red Sea on dry ground? Cry out to God and let Him provide for you.

Prayer

God, part my Red Sea today so that I might walk through the trials of life on dry ground. Make a way for me when it seems there is no way. Thank You, God, for Your miraculous works. Amen.

Redo

Main Text

1 John 1:9: "If we confess our sins, he is faithful and just and will forgive us our sins and purify us from all unrighteousness."

Meditation

Have you ever wondered what it would be like to redo your life, or at least a portion of your life? If you are like me, the thought of being able to redo a portion of your life is appealing. Recently I was teaching a sixth-grade Sunday school class on choosing our words wisely when one of the students said, "Hey, wouldn't it be cool if we could redo something we did wrong and make it right, pretend it never happened?" This young man's idea struck me instantly. He is right. It would really be cool if we could redo scenes in our lives. We have all done things that we are not proud of or we wish we could do over to make it better or to alter the outcome. Unfortunately, in life we do not have this opportunity . . . or do we? First John 1:9 says, "If we confess our sins, he is faithful and just and will forgive us."

What an awesome promise to know that we do have a second chance. Jesus forgives and forgets those things that we have done wrong or may not be so proud of. Even though we do not have a magical Redo button, we are assured of God's unfailing grace.

The next time you wish you could hit the Redo button like the young man in my Sunday school class and do something over, remember that Jesus is the master of "redos" and He is always standing by waiting to forgive and forget. His promise of forgiveness is better than any redo.

Prayer

Father, I ask this day that You forgive me of those things I wish I could redo. Thank You that I know You forgive and forget and that You love me in spite of what I have done. Amen.

Day 55

Speed Need

Main Text

John 16:33: "I have told you these things, so that in me you may have peace. In this world you will have trouble. But take heart! I have overcome the world."

Meditation

I love speed—the faster, the better. My ultimate dream vehicle is a BMW. With its sleek design, low-riding, curve-hugging feel, I am convinced that the BMW was designed with me in mind. Although I will more than likely never own a BMW, I like to fantasize that one day I may.

The fastest open public freeway is the Audubon in Germany. With no legal speed limit, the Audubon allows you to dare your need for speed. Those who have driven the Audubon report a freedom not known by most drivers. No boundaries, no limits, no enforcement of speed rules for all practical purposes. I experienced part of my dream for speed not long ago when I had the opportunity to drive the Audubon and topped my open-road speed at 175 KM. I've been told that's not bad for a first-time Audubon driver.

Although I would have loved to go faster, I was held back by something; other than my wife, that is. I am not sure how to describe it. Although I knew the speed rules of the road were wiped away, I felt constrained and responsible for my actions. Perhaps it was my limited experience of driving that fast or my reluctance to trust that there was not a speed limit and the consequences of my actions would not be punished under law. Whatever the basis, I found myself limiting my speed experience.

All too often, I believe this can be true of our daily lives. Jesus Christ gave His all, His life, for you and me. There is nothing greater and nothing more to give. Yet we find ourselves limiting our actions because we fear or do not trust that Jesus Christ paid it all. John 16:33 says that Jesus Christ has overcome the world. This means no more fear, worry, distrust, anxiety, or other obstacles can limit you. Trust Him today and know that He has overcome.

As for the Audubon, it could only have been better had I rented the BMW. Maybe next time.

Prayer

Father, thank You that You have truly overcome the world and that in You I can be victorious in all that I do. Use me today to make a difference for Your kingdom. In Your beautiful name I pray. Amen.

Day 56

We Don't Know the Time

Main Text

Mark 13:32: "But about that day or hour no one knows, not even the angels in heaven, nor the Son, but only the Father."

Meditation

Remember when you were a little kid and you didn't worry about time. The days ran together as one long, never-ending stretch of time. From morning to night you were free to do whatever you wanted. Then the day came when you went to school and suddenly time could stand still. If you were like me, you remember staring at the clock during school with seemingly no movement by the second hand. Time really did stand still, or so we thought.

Now, as an adult, we know we are given 24 hours a day, or 8,760 hours per year to do all we need to get done. Suddenly we find ourselves without enough time to accomplish all we need to. Incredible how our perspective of time changes depending on where we are in life.

There is a day coming, as promised in Scripture, when we will be taken away to meet the Father in heaven. We don't know when this appointed time and day will be. As I think about the perspective of time and heaven, I recall Mark 13:32, which tells us, "That day or hour no one knows, not even the angels, nor the Son, but only the Father." Even though we do not know the time or the day that we will be whisked away to heaven, we do know that we have a promise of a heaven-bound trip.

Pay attention today how you spend your twenty-four hours. Are you doing and accomplishing what will bring honor to the Father? If not, adjust your time, because we do not know the hour when we may be called away.

Prayer

Jesus, time is short, and I pray that today You will help me make the most of every hour, knowing You have created time and space. Let me keep watch for Your soon return, that I might be ready to meet You. Amen.

Day 57

Voices of Praise

Main Text

Psalm 148:2: "Praise him, all his angels; praise him, all his heavenly hosts."

Meditation

I like to watch sports on television, but enjoy attending sporting events in person even more. I like the roar of the crowd, the energy you feel, and the smells that linger in the air of all my favorite game foods. The thrill of attending a game cannot be adequately described with words; it is one of those things you need to experience for yourself.

Recently I attended an evangelistic service in Orlando, Florida. The service was held in a large sports arena, which held over seventeen thousand spectators, or in this case, seventeen thousand believers in Christ. As I sat in the arena, my mind flashed to the excitement I feel when I attend sporting events, but the excitement in the arena this evening was altogether different. The awesome, holy power of Jesus filled the arena as seventeen thousand brothers and sisters sang praise to Jesus. Psalm 148:2 declares that we "praise him, all his angles; praise him, all his heavenly hosts."

Imagine an arena of believers praising our living Savior. As I stood that evening, with eyes closed, listening, I could not help but wonder what heaven will be like and what the praise to our King will sound like. What I do know is that the praise will be beautiful music to our ears and that all of heaven will erupt in joyous praise. What a day that will be when we witness and experience Jesus face-to-face. Are you ready to be part of God's glorious "heavenly hosts"? I am. I will watch for you there.

Prayer

God, You desire my praise; it is music to Your ears. Let me always praise You and give You glory for Your endless love toward me. Amen.

Can You Trust Me?

Main Text

2 Samuel 7:28: "Sovereign Lord, you are God! Your covenant is trustworthy, and you have promised these good things to your servant."

Meditation

Recently I gave a presentation at a leadership conference to a group of young, energetic, and enthusiastic up-and-coming leaders. What a privilege to help shape the lives of our future community and society leaders.

During the afternoon of our first session, I watched this young group of leaders participate in the team-building exercise called the ropes course. The ropes course is an aerial exercise completed twenty-five feet above the ground where participants are outfitted with ropes and harnesses as they go through a series of trust-related activities. The purpose of the ropes course is to reinforce your ability to trust your teammates by letting them guide you in completing specific actions and maneuvers such as walking on a beam or wire elevated twenty-five feet in the air. As each participant had his or her turn, the reaction was different. Some approached the exercise with confidence, others were apprehensive, and some refused to complete the exercise because their fear was too great.

As I stood on the ground watching, my heart was stirred with strong emotions of fear, excitement, and finally relief as each of these young leaders overcame the hurdles set before them. You see, trusting someone to guide you and lead you in the proper way takes courage and an extreme commitment to others. I recalled 2 Samuel 7:28: ""Sovereign

Lord, you are God! Your covenant is trustworthy." God's awesome promise to us is that we can trust Him in all things and we do not need to worry whether He will be there to guide us. God's Word clearly tells us that if we trust God, He will be with us, regardless of the situation.

Oftentimes we try to place our trust in the hands of others and miss the real trustworthy source of our guidance: Jesus Christ. Trust Jesus today; He will not fail you.

Prayer

Jesus, I pray that You give me courage to trust You in all things, and let me know that You are in control of each and every circumstance in my life. I thank You for the promises found in Your Word. Amen.

Light in the Darkness

Main Text

John 8:12: "When Jesus spoke again to the people, he said, 'I am the light of the world. Whoever follows me will not walk in darkness, but will have the light of life.'"

Meditation

I enjoy early-morning biking when the air is fresh and the streets are quiet. As an early-morning bicyclist, I often start my ride when the sky is dark. In an attempt to help me navigate my way through the darkened streets, my wife recently bought me a new high-tech bicycle light. This light is no ordinary bicycle light, but instead is a new dimension light designed to penetrate the dark morning light and pave the way for safe biking. As I began to use my new high-tech device, the light proved to illuminate my path beyond what I thought possible.

As I rode my bike with my path well lit, I pondered John 8:12, when Jesus said, "I am the Light of the world. Whoever follows me will not walk in darkness." What a tremendous promise Jesus gives to us. The pledge is that if we follow Jesus, we will no longer be in darkness but instead will have our path each and every day illuminated by God's truth.

When I follow God, my path is lit and it is clear as to where I am going. We need to accept and know that Jesus provides us with the ability to see in the darkness; however, we also need to be willing to accept His guidance in our lives to have that light.

Are you willing to turn your dimly lit path into the glorious light of Jesus? Try it. You will find your path much less challenging.

Prayer

Father, help me follow the path You set before me. Let me trust You and know that where You take me, I must follow. Amen.

Run the Race Well

Main Text

Hebrews 12:1–2: "Therefore, since we are surrounded by such a great cloud of witnesses, let us throw off everything that hinders and the sin that so easily entangles. And let us run with perseverance the race marked out for us, fixing our eyes on Jesus, the pioneer and perfecter of faith. For the joy set before him he endured the cross, scorning its shame, and sat down at the right hand of the throne of God."

Meditation

A short time ago I had the opportunity to participate in a local 5K Tough Mudder run. Tough Mudder runs are very popular and bring a new dynamic to running by challenging yourself through a maze of obstacles and hurdles all while running through mud and other ground obstructions. The wave of these Tough Mudder runs is sweeping across the United States and creating excitement and a fresh approach to running competitions. On that morning, nearly eight hundred other mud runners and I set our sights on conquering the muddy course that had been designed for us.

As I was waiting at the starting line, I could not help but think about the challenges that were ahead of me. Not knowing what these obstacles were, I became anxious of the unknown, and then the verse in Hebrews 12:1 came to mind: "Let us run with perseverance the race marked out for us, fixing our eyes on Jesus."

What an awesome comfort Jesus can bring to us in any situation. Often we become fearful and restless not knowing what lies ahead of us. However, with Jesus, we are given the reassurance that He is with us and we can run our daily life race with diligence if we keep our eyes on Him. Regardless of what we face or the bumps in our life, we can be assured that Jesus is with us when we rely on Him.

Jesus was with me through the mud obstacles as I kept my eyes fixed on Him, though I did end up covered with mud from head to toe. I was assured He will be with me during the muddy times in life. I challenge you to run your race with perseverance, keeping your eyes on Jesus, and you too can be confident that He will be with you during the challenging times in your life.

Prayer

God, I know that You have Your eyes on me all the time. Give me the determination to daily seek You. Amen.

Blessed Promise

Main Text

Ephesians 2:8–9: "For it is by grace you have been saved, through faith—and this is not from yourselves, it is the gift of God—not by works, so that no one can boast."

Meditation

There is an old hymn written in 1873 by the famous blind hymn writer Fanny Crosby titled "Blessed Assurance." "Blessed Assurance, Jesus is mine! Oh what a foretaste of glory divine. Heir of salvation, purchase of God, born of His Spirit, washed in His blood. This is my story, this is my song, praising my Savior all the day long. This is my story, this is my song, praising my Savior all the day long."

This old hymn is a classic and has profound meaning in the Christian faith. As you read the words, its weighty message shines through. We have the promise that Jesus is ours as we look to Him and His magnificent being. God purchased us by His death so that we can be saved and live eternally in heaven because of His blood that was shed at the cross.

Powerful and impactful, the blessed assurance of salvation remains true, for it is by grace that we are saved. Christ died on Calvary so that we might have life eternal. He gave us a promise some two thousand years ago that declared our deliverance is through Christ. The gift of salvation is easy to receive because the gift has already been given. In order to receive it, we must be willing to ask. How simple is that? You ask and you receive Christ's redemption and miraculous gift of salvation.

Somehow in our world of complexities and chaos, we have lost the simple gift of salvation. Yet this simple gift changes lives, moves mountains, destroys enemies, and guarantees an eternal life in Christ's kingdom. I encourage you to reach out to Christ and ask Him to change you so you might also sing, "Blessed assurance, Jesus is mine! Oh what a foretaste of glory divine."

Prayer

God, hear my prayer today and touch my life. Change me from the inside out that I might know You, God, and sing all day long about You. I am joyful that I can say with confidence, "Blessed assurance, You are mine." Amen.

Day 62

Faithful or Faithless Trust?

Main Text

Hebrews 11:1–2: "Now faith is confidence in what we hope for and assurance about what we do not see. This is what the ancients were commended for."

Meditation

What is faith? I asked this question to a group of people attending a Bible study and the answers varied significantly. One individual responded that faith is trust, another person said faith is believing without seeing, yet another said faith is hoping for an answer to your need. All great answers, and none were right or wrong. Hebrews 11:1 tells us, "Now faith is confidence in what we hope for and assurance about what we do not see."

Faith is hard. Faith can be tiresome, belaboring, frustrating, exhausting, challenging, wearisome, discouraging, and stands as a test of our trust and belief in God. Although God's Word tells us to have faith, it is difficult when you are facing adversity and the unknown. It is hard to have confidence and to find hope when your child is sick, you have lost your job, or you do not know where your next meal is going to come from. The assurance of things we cannot see tests and stretches us.

I have experienced waiting on God to provide in my life. Each time God sends me on a faith journey, I pray that God will make the journey easier than the one before. I challenge God and say, "God, You know my trust and love for You. Isn't that enough?" In the still, small voice I hear God say, "Just wait. Wait on Me, and trust Me. You have no idea what I am doing. Just wait and trust Me." These are the last words you want to hear as God tests your faith and commitment to Him. I have learned that I don't know what God knows, I can't see what God sees, and I don't have the understanding that God does. I must wait patiently before God, taking my concerns to Him daily in prayer. God listens, God hears, God responds, and I know that when we are faithful to Him, He will be faithful to us.

Stand on God's promise and be confident of what you do not see. Seek Him and ask Him to meet your need. Then, when God meets your need, offer your praise and thankfulness to Him.

Prayer

Father, worthy is Your name. Boost my faith that I might walk in the light of Your will and know without a doubt that You have things in my life fully in control. Amen.

Day 63

Calm Down

Main Text

Jonah 1:11–12: "The sea was getting rougher and rougher. So they asked him, 'What should we do to you to make the sea calm down for us?' 'Pick me up and throw me into the sea,' he replied, 'and it will become calm. I know that it is my fault that this great storm has come upon you.'"

Meditation

A few years ago my wife and I took a trip to the Island of St. Martin. One of the things on our bucket list was to go deep-sea fishing. I wanted to catch the "big one." It was a beautiful day, a clear bright-blue sky, the sun coming up on the horizon . . . the makings of a perfect fishing day at sea. We boarded the fishing vessel, received our instruction from our fishing captain, and headed out to sea. The water was calm eight miles out into ocean and the conditions were perfect as we began our fishing adventure. Perfect, that is, until an hour into our fishing excursion, when out of nowhere the wind began to blow and the ocean waves began to crest. I will confess this was one of the most frightening experiences of my life. We tossed and turned, thrashed up and down, and bounced across the ocean waves as we sluggishly made our way back to shore. Some in the fishing vessel became violently ill and were stricken with vomiting and severe nausea. The captain of our vessel did all he could to get us back to shore safely.

I remember exiting the fishing vessel when we finally made it back to shore. I too was ill. I recall lying on the pier with the world spinning around me and my stomach in my throat. It took me quite some time to get my land legs back. In that moment, I was reminded of the Bible story of Jonah and the whale. Jonah was running from God because he did not want to do what God had asked him to do. So Jonah decided to run as far away as possible from the work God had laid before him. Jonah found himself in a predicament of a violent storm on the sea, much like the one I experienced, because of his disobedience. With no other choice, Jonah's shipmates were forced to throw him into the sea. The Bible tells us, "Then they took Jonah and threw him overboard, and the raging sea grew calm" (Jonah 1:15). What a powerful thing, to know that God controls every step of our lives. We can try and run, but God sees and knows all. God had bigger plans for Jonah, one that included a three-day stay inside the belly of a fish. You see, God had to capture Jonah's attention and help him focus on the work He had set before him.

What is God trying to capture in your life? Surrender to God; take the risk to see where He is leading you. Like Jonah, God may be trying to get your attention. Submit to Jesus, or you too may find yourself with a three-day stay at the "Whale Inn." God may have an adventure you cannot pass up. Take the risk.

Prayer

Father, give me the courage this day to accomplish the task You set before me. Let me go boldly into the world to do what You desire of me today. Amen.

Face Lift

Main Text

Acts 4:12: "Salvation is found in no one else, for there is no other name under heaven given to mankind by which we must be saved."

Meditation

I enjoy painting. Any kind of painting: the inside of a room, the side of a building, it doesn't matter what it is. I find painting to be therapeutic in nature, though I am not altogether sure why. As a child, I grew up on a dairy farm that had many buildings on the farm homestead. I can recall each summer selecting a building to paint. There was something about the preparation work of scraping the old paint off, priming the building, and painting the building that brought a sense of completion to my mind. My parents always said they had the nicest-looking farm in the whole county because the buildings were perfectly painted.

I can remember the preparation process as I began my annual summer painting. It was a lot of work to scrape off the old paint and sand any boards that needed a bit of restoration. I always felt as though the building standing in its stripped state was the worst a building could look. But I knew that the old paint needed to come off before the primer could go on. Once I brushed on the primer, the building began to take a different look; it went from an ugly, stained look to a dull, faint hue of white, to a gray. However, after the primer came the bright white coat of fresh paint. The first few stokes of my brush beamed brightly against the dull gray primer. It was as though the building glowed as the sun glistened against the fresh paint. I loved that look. It transformed the building from dismal to radiant.

As I reflect back on my summer painting projects, it reminds me of what Christ has done in my life. He took my old, rundown soul, scraped away the chipped and weathered paint, then brushed on a fresh coat of primer, and finally covered my sins with a brilliant white paint. In short, Christ redeemed my life and gave me newness from the inside out. No longer was I gray and dingy and in need of repair. Instead, Christ covered it all with one stroke of His redemptive blood from His death on the cross. Christ died and rose again that we might have eternal life.

The concept of Christ dying on a cross and giving His life for me is difficult to understand. Who am I that Christ would die for me? Because of Christ's death, I have become a child of the King, Christ Jesus.

Prayer

Father, thank You for giving me new life, for stripping away the old chipped paint and making me white as snow in Your sight. Take my life and use me to make a difference in the lives of those I come in contact with. Amen.

Day 65

Leadership Hero

Main Text

Numbers 27:18: "So the LORD said to Moses, 'Take Joshua son of Nun, a man in whom is the spirit of leadership, and lay your hand on him.'"

Meditation

If I were to ask you who your leader hero is, who would you say? JFK, the president of the United States, a parent, a grandparent? Who would you pick? A website listing the all-time greatest leaders in history has recorded Mahatma Gandhi, Nelson Mandala, Martin Luther King Jr., Abraham Lincoln, and Mao Zedong. Some of these names you may recognize while others are a bit more unknown. One thing that these great leaders all had in common was their drive and determination to generate change. That frightening word, *change*, is the most shared trait that has created great leaders.

In our society, we have an overabundance of information on what creates a great leader. Some say great leaders are born while others believe leaders are made. Others define a great leader as one who is a risk taker, a great communicator, arrogant, trustworthy, a visionary. Whatever quality you choose to identify as a great leader is up to you.

When I think about biblical leaders, I think of Moses, the leader of Israelites. Moses used impressive skills to lead God's anointed people. Moses' leadership abilities were divinely appointed and inspired by God Himself. Although Moses did not believe he had the necessary skills to lead the Israelites, God intervened on his behalf and provided ability beyond Moses' natural skill set. How about Joshua, a strong ally of Moses? Joshua was an outstanding and obedient follower of Moses, who waited patiently until it was his time to lead the Israelites. Joshua was known as the strong leader of Israel as the Israelites conquered the land God promised to them. Then there was David, a leader who was sensitive to the call of God in his life. David recognized that his strength and skill came from God and God alone. In the Psalms we can hear the voice of David as he cried out to God, seeking His direction and help. Then there was Daniel. We see Daniel promoted to positions of power and influence under the reign of King Nebuchadnezzar. Daniel's influence helped shape the course of history as he sought after God's divine inspiration.

The common theme in each of these biblical leaders was the divine intervention of God in their lives. The raw trust gave them confidence to lead people, lead a nation, and eventually impact the human race. As I ponder this concept, it is difficult for me to grasp. Do you think that these leaders knew the magnitude of their tasks? Did they have any understanding of what God was doing through them? I don't know the answers to these questions. What I do know is that God uses ordinary people with ordinary skills who are willing to take a risk and seek change.

Has God called you to leadership? If so, then lead. If God is tugging at your heart to engage, then respond to His call. What if you were called to be the next Moses, Joshua, David, or Daniel? Are you ready to lead? Would you be willing to seek the face of God? Could you resist your own will and provide the direction and leadership as asked by God? For every great leader, there is a submissive heart aligned and filled with God's Spirit. Is God calling you to lead?

Prayer

Father, create in me a leadership heart that I might lead according to Your will and create change that influences Your kingdom. Help me lead with integrity and skill. Amen.

Day 66

Open Communication

Main Text

2 Chronicles 6:19: "Yet, LORD my God, give attention to your servant's prayer and his plea for mercy. Hear the cry and the prayer that your servant is praying in your presence."

Meditation

If your cell phone service is like mine, sometimes you have coverage and sometimes you don't. It never fails that when I need cell phone service the most is when I have the greatest difficulty staying connected. In fact, just recently we changed cell phone providers because of poor, inconsistent service. After doing my research and comparing plans of several major providers, we made the change to a new carrier. With this change, we were promised outstanding service in all of the spaces and places we journey on a daily basis. The concept of having reliable service was intriguing to us and would be a welcome change. At first, our new provider proved to have good coverage wherever we found ourselves. How nice. Then the problem came. I think you know where this is heading. The dreaded hour arrived when I needed service at a critical time and had no connectivity. Nothing. No tower strength, no texting, and no data service. I was completely without communication.

As I scrambled to find a location where I could make my phone conference, it occurred to me that regardless of how reliable our communication service might seem, there is always the potential of no service. I was reminded of the communication between Christ and us. The channel of communication is always open, always live, and always dependable in any circumstance and in any location. Communicating with Christ is simple; it's called prayer. In Solomon's prayer at the temple dedication in 2 Chronicles 6:19, we hear Solomon pray, "LORD my God, give attention to your servant's prayer and his plea for mercy. Hear the cry and the prayer that your servant is praying in your presence."

We too need to seek Christ daily. We need to bring our petitions before Him and pray as Solomon did, asking God to hear our cry. When we pray, I believe God listens. Scripture is clear that God does hear our pleas and desires our praise. What need do you have? Have you spent time in letting God know your needs? My friend, I can assure you that God does answer our petitions. Many times God does not answer our prayers as we might expect, but He does meet our need. Sometimes God delays His answer and sometimes He changes direction or changes our hearts and our attitudes. But He is always there, always in touch with us. We may not like God's answer, but He knows what is best for us. Bow your heart, and let Christ know your need.

Prayer

Father, I pray this day that You hear my cry and prayer and that You meet me where I am. I need You more today than any other day. Please come and help me through this day. Amen.

Walk in It

Main Text

Isaiah 30:21: "Whether you turn to the right or to the left, your ears will hear a voice behind you, saying, 'This is the way; walk in it.'"

Meditation

Isaiah 30 talks of the approaching danger of Jerusalem and desolations of Judah by King Sennacherib's invasion. This chapter speaks of a gracious promise to those who trust in God: if they make it through their troubled times, happier days will follow.

This sounds like our lives, doesn't it? How often do we find ourselves in the same situation? Trouble is rising up all around us, and we feel as though we are sinking and that the end seems like it will never come. We cling to the hope that when this trouble passes, only happier days will follow. Life is challenging and filled with uncountable pressures, stresses, and calamities that seem to mount all around us. We ponder how we will get through the test that God has set before us. We question, "Why me, God? What did I do to justify my troubles?" Our list of "whys" is endless.

My friends, the beauty of God's grace is sufficient to take us through whatever blow stands in our path. Isaiah 30:21 declares, "Whether you turn to the right or to the left, your ears will hear a voice behind you, saying, this is the way; walk in it." This verse has special meaning to me as I stand on God's promise to see me through troubles in my life. Often, we are so busy battling in our situation that we fail to hear the voice of God. We are pulled in many directions, believing that if we turn to the right, we will find resolve. Perhaps if we turn to the left, our troubles will subside. Oh, but then you seek God and suddenly "hear a voice behind you, saying, 'This is the way; walk in it.'"

How powerful to know that we can hear God's voice. Sometimes He whispers and sometimes He shouts. However God speaks to you, there is an assurance that if we follow God's voice, we will know the way to walk. We will know what to do and God will lead us. Are you struggling to hear God? Are you looking to the right or to the left and remain unsure what to do? Pause, seek God, and then listen for His direction. God has happier days planned for your life. God's Word declares it. Now practice what we are instructed to do: walk in it.

Prayer

God, help me listen to Your voice and know where to walk. Do not let me turn to the right or left, but instead, follow You. Thank You, God, that You are speaking to me. Give me ears to hear Your voice. Amen.

The Eyes Have It

Main Text

1 Corinthians 15:52: "In a flash, in the twinkling of an eye, at the last trumpet. For the trumpet will sound, the dead will be raised imperishable, and we will be changed."

Meditation

Have you ever thought about your eyes? Your eyes have color and tears, are used to see with and blink, and are the fastest muscle found in the human body. You have heard the old phrase "in a blink of an eye"; well, now you know where the phrase came from. Our eyes blink, on average, twenty times per minute or nearly twenty-nine thousand times per day. Any guess as to the most common eye color in the world? The browns have it with approximately 55 percent of the world population being brown-eyed.

The eye is an incredible muscle in the body and one that we often take for granted. Worldwide, it is estimated that 180 million people are blind or visually impaired. Then there is a percentage of the population like me who are colorblind. It's not good to be colorblind. Our world relies on way too many colors and color-related schemes. You might hear me say something like, "I really like that blue color." My wife will immediately correct me and say, "You mean that purple color?" Blue, purple, it's all the same to me.

Eyes bring our world to life and allow us to take in the sights around us. First Corinthians 15:52 declares that there is day coming when "in a flash, in the twinkling of an eye" Jesus Christ will come back to earth to take all believers to heaven to live there with Him for an eternity.

Think about that moment—that mere blink in time when we will be gone, vanished from earth. As I ponder this, I am absolutely captivated that such an act could take place. One moment people will be going about their daily business and then suddenly—gone, taken away to be with our Savior, Jesus Christ.

There are brothers and sisters in Christ all around our world. In that moment, in that blink, people from every nation and every tribe will be disappear from this world. Imagine the stir that will be created when the world fully understands the full meaning of "in a flash, in the twinkling of an eye." Are you ready to make the journey in a blink of an eye?

Prayer

Jesus, I am ready for the moment, for the blink of an eye when You come to take me to heaven. Let me share Your good news with others so that they too can say, "I am ready, in a blink of an eye." Amen.

Day 69

Celebrating Life

Main Text

Psalm 90:12: "Teach us to number our days, that we may gain a heart of wisdom."

Meditation

My father will celebrate his eightieth birthday in just a few days, and my siblings and I are planning a huge birthday party. Family and friends whom my father has not seen in several years will be coming to the party. Special entertainment, food, decorations, music, and of course, stories of the past will all be part of the celebration. Reaching a milestone of celebrating eighty years of life is a big deal and is certainly worthy of a party. I am not quite sure how we are going to get eighty candles on the birthday cake and all lit at the same time, however.

All around the world celebrations of birthdays is a tradition. Regardless of age, we each enjoy the laughter and fun of family and friends as we share in the birthday custom with cake and ice cream. Psalm 90:12–14 says, "Teach us to number our days, that we may get a heart of wisdom. . . . Satisfy us in the morning with your steadfast love, that we may rejoice and be glad all our days." This psalm is a prayer of Moses as he reflected on God's grace. How fitting that we seek a heart of wisdom from God. May God show us His steadfast love so that each day we may rejoice and be glad for what He has done for us. You see, we are all saved by Christ's grace; none are exempt. We are to search for Christ's wisdom and grace that He abundantly provides to us. It is our honor and our duty, as we serve Christ, to seek after His steadfast love so that we may share His love with others.

Misao Okawa, a Japanese woman, is considered to be the oldest woman alive today, at the age of 116. What an incredible feat to celebrate her 116th birthday. As I think about this, I cannot help but wonder that if we reached the age of 116, what influence for the kingdom of Christ we might have made. Will we have helped to change the world, preached the gospel, led others to Christ, helped train pastors, or financially supported missionaries? Or will we have sat on the sidelines, hopeful that someone else answered the call to influence others for the kingdom of Christ? Take courage this day and seek God's wisdom and steadfast love so that you may rejoice all your days. Celebrate your birthday this year in a big way.

Prayer

God, teach me Your ways so that I might gain a heart of wisdom. Let me experience Your love to influence others for You. Amen.

On the Scene

Main Text

Genesis 6:13: "So God said to Noah, 'I am going to put an end to all people, for the earth is filled with violence because of them. I am surely going to destroy both them and the earth.'"

Meditation

I love to watch the news. For whatever reason, I am completely fascinated by the fact that I can travel around the world in a thirty-minute newscast. Watching a live news report on the Gulf of Mexico as the results of a devastating hurricane are revealed. Learning of the violence in Afghanistan as our military patrols the war-torn country. Viewing events in Washington, DC, as the president of the United States is about to address the nation. Our world has become much smaller than what we knew just a decade ago. Technology allows us to see and feel the raw emotion and elements of mankind from around the globe. Sometimes it's frightening to me.

There was a man in the Bible by the name of Noah. I am sure you are familiar with the story of Noah and the ark. Noah was a godly man who walked by faith and trusted in God. Scripture reports that God saw that the world had become corrupt and full of violence and the people were immoral. God had a plan, however, and this plan included Noah. God said to Noah in Genesis 6:13, "I am going to put an end to all people, for the earth is filled with violence because of them." What do you think Noah was feeling as God told him His plan? Fear, disbelief, confusion, excitement, anger? We are not sure. Scripture does not tell us what Noah's initial response was. What we do know is that Noah was obedient and fulfilled the instructions God gave him. If God had come to me and told me to build an ark because of the corruption of people and said that He was going to destroy the entire world, I am not sure how I would have responded. Noah, being the godly man he was, responded just as God knew he would, with meekness and submission to God's plan.

We all know the rest of the story. Noah built the ark with specific instruction given by God in terms of size, materials, height, and features of the ark. He collected the supplies necessary for the ark's journey and gathered two of every animal. No detail was forgotten, left out, or altered in any way. It was God's plan, and there was no room for change. We too must not alter the plans God has for us. We may think we know what is best or how to do something better, but the cold, hard reality is that we must be diligent in honoring what God has put before us.

Are you ready to build an ark?

Prayer

Father, let me see things as You see them and understand as You do. Use me to accomplish Your plans. Amen.

Wind, Be Still

Main Text

Mark 4:39–40: "And he got up, rebuked the wind and said to the waves, 'Quiet! Be still!' Then the wind died down and it was completely calm. He said to his disciples, 'Why are you so afraid? Do you still have no faith?'"

Meditation

If you have ever driven through southwest Minnesota, you have no doubt seen the wind turbine farms. Acre after acre of land is covered by rows of massive wind turbines neatly lined up in formation. It is actually quite an awesome sight. These large wind turbines, sometimes called windmills, are alternative-power generation systems. Each turbine stands 229 feet tall, has blades that span 136 feet, and has a base that is 16 feet in diameter. At the optimum wind speed of 25–35 mph, the mammoth blades rotate at 14 mph, generating power that is carried across the Midwest. Each tower can power approximately five hundred households for a year. Did I mention the price tag per tower is $2.5 million?

Not long ago, I had the opportunity to stand with my brother-in-law at the base of one of these giant energy-producing towers. It was an impressive sight. The thing that stands out most in my mind was the whisper of the wind from the rotating blades. It was a peaceful, calming sound that echoed far across the ridge where we stood as we watched the blades turn in unison.

Mark 4 tells of another wind, a wind that was not so peaceful. Jesus and His disciples had just finished preaching when they decided to cross the Sea of Galilee and minister on other side of the sea shore. Exhausted from the day, Jesus had fallen asleep while His disciples manned the boat. Out of nowhere, "a furious squall came up, and the waves broke over the boat, so that it was nearly swamped" (v. 37). Frightened and not knowing what to do, the disciples decided to wake Jesus.

Jesus awoke and rebuked the wind. He said to the sea, "Quiet! Be still!" (v. 39). At Jesus' command, the wind stopped and the sea returned to normal. How can you not be moved at the miraculous hand of Jesus that even the wind and sea obey Him? What a mighty display of Jesus' power, a power that is available to us as we journey through life. We serve Jesus, the wind and sea tamer.

Prayer

Father, please come and calm the wind on the sea of my life. Let me hear You say, "Quiet! Be still!" Amen.

Day 72

It's All in the Foundation

Main Text

Matthew 7:25: "The rain came down, the streams rose, and the winds blew and beat against that house; yet it did not fall, because it had its foundation on the rock."

Meditation

My wife and I have been privileged to live in three new homes since we have been married. We were heavily involved in the last home we built in terms of designing, planning, and picking out materials and colors. Even though we say we were involved in the process, neither my wife nor I did any of the actual construction. There are obvious reasons for that. Instead, we chose a well-qualified contractor with a good reputation whom we knew would build the home exactly to our specifications. More importantly, however, we knew that the builder would not take shortcuts that could alter the home's structure. We did all the right things by choosing the land, making plans, interviewing the contractor, and then trusting the builder to carry out the plan.

Jesus often taught in parables so the people could understand and grasp a concept or idea. Jesus also spoke of building a solid foundation on the rock. In Mark 7:25, Jesus said, "The rain came down, the streams rose, and the winds blew and beat against that house; yet it did not fall, because it had its foundation on the rock." What was Jesus really trying to say in this parable? Jesus was teaching that in order to have your house stand through storms, you need to build your home on rock, not sand. Jesus is referring to your heart and the importance of accepting Him as your Savior. Sand, as we all know, gives way when the rain comes.

Think of the sand castles you build at the beach. The tide comes in, and when the water recedes, it carries the sand back into the sea.

The same is true in our lives. If we trust in the One who can build a strong foundation, then we will have a reliable and sturdy base, and can be assured that we will live a life filled with joy, happiness, and contentment. This strong foundation is Jesus. If we choose not to live for Jesus, our lives will be built on a foundation that is not sturdy, offers despair, lacks trust, and holds no future. On which foundation have you built your life? One that offers hope or one that offers uncertainty? If you have not asked Jesus to come into your life, do it today. A simple prayer asking Jesus to change your life is all it takes. "The rain came down, the streams rose, and the winds blew and beat against that house; yet it did not fall, because it had its foundation on the rock."

Prayer

Jesus, thank You that I have built my foundation on You, the solid Rock. I know that when the wind comes and the storm rages, You will be there. Amen.

Day 73

Preparation

Main Text

Matthew 13:33: "He told them still another parable: 'The kingdom of heaven is like yeast that a woman took and mixed into about sixty pounds of flour until it worked all through the dough.'"

Meditation

My wife has this crazy bread maker that she uses on very rare occasions. For whatever reason, this machine gets under my skin. Maybe because it's old, discolored, and makes the most awful sounds. My wife spends time looking through recipe books, measuring, pouring, and sifting, when she could have simply bought a fresh baked loaf of bread from the grocery store. But each time she uses the machine, it's the same outcome. After the mess, after the noise, and after the cleanup, you can smell the fresh bread baking throughout the entire house. It's a sweet aroma that penetrates your nostrils and excites your taste buds. It is in those moments when my wife likes to remind me that perhaps I shouldn't complain about the machine so much.

One of the ingredients in bread is yeast. Yeast is a microorganism from the fungi family. Sounds yummy, doesn't it? This little microorganism is responsible for infecting a batch of dough. From this infection, the bread dough expands, or rises. Preaching the gospel is a lot like yeast. As Jesus taught yet another parable, He used yeast as the basis for His story. Yeast is like the Word of God working in the hearts of people who receive Him. We cannot see it, but we know that the love of Christ is in our hearts. By sharing the gospel of Christ, we are spreading the good news of Jesus Christ.

Matthew 13:33 says, "The kingdom of heaven is like yeast that a woman took and mixed into about sixty pounds of flour until it is worked all through the dough." Just like the woman who mixed yeast into her bread dough, we are to share the gospel diligently with others so that the kingdom of heaven can expand. That means more lost souls will come to know the saving grace of Jesus Christ.

The next time you smell the sweet aroma of fresh bread, let this scripture be etched on your mind as you spread the power of Christ to those you meet.

Prayer

Jesus, please use me to spread Your good news to those I come in contact with today. Let me mix the yeast of Your Holy Spirit in the lives of others. Amen.

Prayers of the Saints

Main Text

1 John 5:14–15: "And this is the confidence we have in approaching God: that if we ask anything according to his will, he hears us. And if we know that he hears us—whatever we ask—we know that we have what we asked of him."

Meditation

Today a revelation came to me as I was visiting with a dear saint in Christ who has faithfully served God for nearly sixty-five years. I was sharing with him a concern going on in my life and how I was trusting God to intervene on my behalf. He stopped me midway through my sharing and said, "I want you to know that I have been praying for you and that I believe there is power in prayer." Did you hear that? "There is power in prayer." My friend, I want you to know more than ever that there truly is power in prayer. I cannot begin to tell you the ways in which Christ Jesus has intervened in my life. Prayer is one of the mysteries of God that we will never know or be able to understand its significance.

Prayer moves mountains and heals deaf ears, blind eyes, and lame limbs. Prayer calms raging seas and brings the dead to life. Prayer heals broken marriages, restores families, and heals the hurt between a mother and daughter or a father and son. Prayer binds the enemy's attacks and provides employment and meets our financial needs. Prayer brings restoration, deliverance, and forgiveness. Prayer protects, guides, leads, and empowers us to live victorious lives through the redemptive blood that was shed on Calvary by Jesus Christ for you and me.

I was completely unprepared to hear the words spoken by my dear friend. "There is power in prayer" echoed in my mind all day. You see, I know there is power in prayer. I've experienced God's power. Even though we know and believe that there is power in prayer, we need to be reminded of this by those who are standing in the gap on our behalf by praying for us. We need to encourage each other and build each other up in prayer, knowing that God is our Deliverer.

Just like this dear saint who is standing in the gap on my behalf, interceding to the Father, I pray that you stand in the gap for someone in need or someone God places on your heart. We may never know the outcome of our prayers for others, but we can be assured that God does answer prayer and that He is a faithful God.

First John 5:14–15 reminds us, "And if we know that he hears us— whatever we ask—we know that we have what we have asked of him."

Prayer

Father, You are my God who hears my prayers. You not only hear my prayers, but You respond with grace and power on my behalf. Thank You for the dear saints of God who intercede for me. Amen.

And the Beat Goes On

Main Text

Psalm 33:2: "Praise the LORD with the harp; make music to him on the ten-stringed lyre."

Meditation

Can you name the 1,264 music genres that exist in the world? Country, rock, classical, gospel, jazz, rap, R&B, Latin, blues, hip-hop . . . Music is a worldwide common denominator that brings nations and people of all ages together, and it is a powerful media that can touch hearts and bring tears to eyes. Jubal is named in Genesis 4:21 as the inventor of musical instruments. The harp and the flute are specifically named as the first instruments known to man. Imagine that the harp and flute were first played by Jubal, a descendant of Cain, the son of Lamech.

We read of David playing the harp, horns sounding as the men marched around the wall of Jericho, and trumpets announcing our final earthly call as Jesus Christ returns to earth to take us to heaven. Throughout Scripture we read and experience music and song. "Shout for joy to the Lord, all the earth, burst into jubilant song with music" (Psalm 98:4). "Let the message of Christ dwell among you richly as you teach and admonish one another with all the wisdom through psalms, hymns, and songs from the Spirit, singing to God with gratitude in your hearts" (Colossians 3:16).

God declares that we are to praise Him, dance before Him, and make beautiful noise unto the Lord. This is not a request or a suggestion. It is God's direction to us that we are to worship Him on instruments and with a shout of praise. How much does God love our worship? So much so that God created music and worship to fill our soul with thanksgiving and praise. Worship Christ today in song and on instrument. Christ desires your praise; shout it out regardless of what you may sound like or how well you play an instrument. God created music, so whatever talent you have, use it for His kingdom's sake.

Opera, reggae, easy listening, honky-tonk, heavy metal . . . 1,249 more genres to name.

Prayer

Father, thank You that You have created music for me to enjoy. Let me sing, dance, shout, and worship You with music. Let my praise be sweet music to Your ears. Amen.

Black with White Stripes or White with Black Stripes?

Main Text

Job 11:7: "Can you fathom the mysteries of God? Can you probe the limits of the Almighty?"

Meditation

Is a zebra black with white stripes or white with black strips? Good question, right? Many zoologists would say that a zebra is white because its stripes end toward the belly and the belly is almost entirely white. Others would say that a zebra is black because if you shaved all the fur off a zebra, the skin is almost completely black. So it really depends on how you look at it. I love mind-bending puzzles and mysteries like this. They cause me to think differently and explore the possibilities, but there are many people who are content with the mystery.

In Job 11, we read of a conversation Job has with Zophar. Zophar is dogmatic and narrow in his thinking and poses rhetorical questions about God. Job 11:7–9 says, "Can you fathom the mysteries of God? Can you probe the limits of the Almighty? They are higher than the heavens above—what can you do? They are deeper than the depths below—what can you know? Their measure is longer than the earth and wider than the sea." These are exacting questions, ones that need to be contemplated and meditated on. Can we fathom the mysteries of God? God is all powerful, controls all, created all, and is the supreme being of heaven and earth. Are there limits to the Almighty? As King over all, He knows no limits or boundaries. Who are we to question the authority of God?

When I contemplate who God is, I stand in awe of the wonder of who He is and what He has done in my life. There is no other and there can be no other than Jesus Christ. I may ponder the mysteries of who God is, but I will never understand the wholeness of God. One day when I get to heaven, I believe God will reveal some of the mysteries that have occupied my mind. Until then, I will bask in the awe-inspiring mysteries of who God is by trusting in His unfailing love and grace.

Prayer

Father, I look toward the day when You reveal the mysteries of who You are. I pray that You give me a mind to understand and the ability to know You more each day. Amen.

A Servant's Heart

Main Text

John 13:5: "He poured water into a basin and began to wash his disciples' feet, drying them with the towel that was wrapped around him."

Meditation

How many pairs of shoes do you own? I recently read a survey that had asked how many pairs of shoes the average American man and women owned. You might be surprised to learn that the average American man owns twelve pairs of shoes while the average American women owns a whopping twenty-seven pairs of shoes. Even more interesting is the fact that the average American man wears three pairs on a routine basis while women wear seven pairs on a routine basis.

Have you ever wondered what being the hands and feet of Jesus means? I suspect it is much more that taking inventory of the shoes we own, or in biblical days, the number of sandals you owned. Jesus calls us to be His hands and feet and share the gospel with those who have not heard the good news. How we serve, whom we serve, why we serve, and the attitude with which we serve others and represent Christ are how we are being the hands and feet of Christ. Jesus Himself presented us with the perfect model to serve others by demonstrating the act of servanthood when He washed the feet of His disciples. He served others to show us His love and teach us how to serve. As children of Christ, we are to model His behavior.

What will you do today to model Christ's servant attitude? As you go about your day, look for ways to serve others. Is it taking your ill neighbor a meal? Running an errand for a friend or family member?

How about volunteering your time at a local food pantry? I know your kid's school needs classroom helpers to be role models for the students. Have you volunteered your time? Your church has asked you to serve, but you offered the excuse that you had too many things going on right now. What if Christ would have offered the same excuse? I understand life is filled with work, school, and other activities, but the real test of service is where we choose to spend our time. Where you give of your time reflects the attitudes of your heart.

Choose to serve. I can promise you that you will not regret one moment of time that you helped share your witness of Christ. Serve Him faithfully and well.

Prayer

God, help me serve You where You call me. Let me give selflessly to others that they might come to know You as their Savior. Amen.

In Search of Your Blanket

Main Text

Nahum 1:7: "The LORD is good, a refuge in times of trouble. He cares for those who trust in him."

Meditation

I find it fascinating to watch little children with their blankets. It is always entertaining. A child's favorite blanket is a precious tool that is used in many circumstances and in many ways. Children sleep with their blanket, play with their blanket, pretend to be superheroes with their blanket, and eat with their blanket. I can remember a time when my wife and I were eating dinner in a local restaurant, and there was a child about the age of three who was having a rough night because mom could not find his blanket. Those poor parents. You know what I mean; you may have found yourself in this same predicament a time or two. The family had just settled in their chairs for what they had hoped would be a peaceful dinner, when all at once their son determined his priceless blanket was missing. Panic and fear set in on the mother's face. Frantically, she searched her purse and the bag she was carrying. Her husband retreated to the car in continued search.

Ah, victory! Dad saved the meal. The blanket was found in the car. The crisis was averted, the meal continued, the son was happy, and the parents were overjoyed. Imagine if the blanket had not been in the car. This family's pleasant experience could have turned ugly quickly.

As I replayed that scene in my mind, I determined that we as adults are just like that three-year-old who had misplaced his blanket. The son knew where to go and whom to turn to when things got tough and something was wrong: mom and dad. We too are like that. Things are good, life is happy, and then all at once, your blanket is missing. Troubles raise their ugly head and rear up all around you. You know what I am saying. Your troubles may not be life and death, but at the moment you are experiencing them, it is overwhelming. Your car breaks down, or your child is home ill for three days when your calendar is filled to overflowing. Your daughter is failing junior high, and you are in despair as to what to do. Your in-laws announce they are coming for a visit. Troubles pick the most inopportune time to strike and often discourage us from being all that God has called us to be.

I so appreciate the verse in Nahum 1:7 that says, "The LORD is good, a refuge in times of trouble. He cares for those who trust in him." You see, troubles come in all sorts of shapes and sizes and are not a respecter of persons. It's called life. How we handle our troubles demonstrates in whom we trust. The Lord is good, and He is a refuge in our times of trouble. Spend a bit of time in prayer today and share with God what is on your heart. Once you share with your heavenly Father, I am confident your missing blanket will be found.

Prayer

Father, I am so glad that I can call on You in times of trouble. I know You not only hear but You respond when I call out to You. Help me today to seek You. Amen.

Does That Make Cents?

Main Text

1 Timothy 6:18–19: "Command them to do good, to be rich in good works, and to be generous and willing to share. In this way they will lay up treasure for themselves as a firm foundation for the coming age, so that they may take hold of the life that is truly life."

Meditation

How many credit card offers do you get in the mail every week? Without exaggeration, I receive an average of ten credit card offers a week. That is 520 credit applications in a year. Just how many credit cards could one possibly need? The average American credit card debt is $15,611. Do you think there is a correlation between credit card mailers and credit card debt? Incredible.

Proverbs 22:7 gives us some wise words to live by: "The rich rule over the poor, and the borrower is slave to the lender." In other words, the Bible is telling us that when we have significant debt, the debt rules our lives and those who give us the money become our masters. My desire is to be free of debt and live a life of prosperity and independence from financial institutions. God gives us a mind to rationalize what we must do to meet our physical needs. Often this means borrowing money and going into debt. However, at the same time, God asks that we be wise with our money and repay what we owe quickly to avoid paying any more interest than necessary. I know people who are determined that borrowing money is a bad thing. I am not sure I agree with this thinking. There are times in life that most of us will need to borrow money, perhaps to buy a home or a vehicle. These are necessities of life.

What is required of us is to be responsible and live within our means so we do not become masters to our money.

I believe God has blessed us with things He desires us to have, but we must be accountable and good stewards. If our money runs our lives, we become slaves to our financial master. Dream for a moment what your money could do if you had no debt? First Timothy 6:18–19 says, "Command them to do good, to be rich in good deeds, and to be generous and willing to share. In this way they will lay up treasure for themselves as a firm foundation for the coming age, so that they may take hold of the life that is truly life."

Be generous with your money. Give to the work of the Lord so that your investment in the kingdom of God will yield many souls for Christ.

Prayer

Jesus, thank You for Your blessings and meeting my financial needs. Help me not be a slave to the money You have given to me. Amen.

Necessary Encounters

Main Text

1 Corinthians 11:25–26: "In the same way, after supper he took the cup, saying, 'This cup is the new covenant in my blood; do this, whenever you drink it, in remembrance of me.' For whenever you eat this bread and drink this cup, you proclaim the Lord's death until he comes."

Meditation

I dislike going to the dentist a great deal. I realize there are probably many people who are like me and do not like the dentist chair experience. The smell, the noise, the taste, or the atmosphere, I am not sure which is more bothersome to me. Perhaps it's the whole experience. Whatever the case, I know that the dentist causes me some distress. However, it is one of the necessary encounters that we must each endure.

Life requires many necessary encounters we do not like. For instance, standing in line at the post office, grocery store, gas station, or restaurant. If we want something or need something, there is often a commitment or a sacrifice that needs to be made. We sacrifice our time at the gym to stay fit and maintain a healthy weight. We sacrifice that extra piece of dessert or sacrifice to buy that new television. Or perhaps you are sacrificing so your child can go to a private school or take piano lessons. Whatever sacrifices you make, you believe they are best for you and your family.

Christ Jesus made the ultimate sacrifice by giving His life that we might have life eternal. When I encounter people who question if there is a God, I cannot help but wonder how they could ever consider making such a statement. Who do they think created the heavens and the earth, the land and the seas, air, wind, sun, food, and water? Who gives them breath? Jesus Christ, that's who. The Giver of Life who sacrificed His own life for you and me. I cannot begin to fathom the breadth and depth of Christ's love for us that He was willing to give His all.

As you ponder the sacrifices you are making, keep them in perspective in comparison to what Jesus gave for you. "In the same way, after supper he took the cup, saying, 'This cup is the new covenant in my blood; do this, whenever you drink it, in remembrance of me.' For whenever you eat this bread and drink the cup, you proclaim the Lord's death until he comes" (1 Corinthians 11:25–26). Rejoice today, my friend, and remember Christ's sacrifice until we meet Him face-to-face.

Prayer

God, Your sacrifice for me was undeserved. You gave all for me that I might spend eternity with You. Please use me this day and every day to advance Your gospel. Thank You, God, for giving Your life for me. Amen.

All in Season

Main Text

Ecclesiastes 3:1: "There is a time for everything, and a season for every activity under the heavens."

Meditation

I live in the beautiful Midwest where I have the privilege of enjoying all four seasons. I like the changes of each season and the newness and freshness that abounds. Winter has its beauty of the freshly fallen snow and sharp crispness in the air. Spring brings new life and new beginnings as the trees, grass, flowers, and other vegetation begin to sprout. Summer continues the lush beauty of spring by bringing full circle the striking blue sky, warm, radiating sunshine, and the cool summer breezes. Fall. Ah, fall, my truly favorite time of the year. There is a keen freshness in the air as summer begins to make its exit and the trees begin to turn their radiant colors of splendor. The air becomes new and has a hint of coolness in the evening with a hint of warmth by day. If you have never seen the Midwest in the fall, it is a road trip worth taking; it's breathtaking.

Scripture reminds us that there is a season for everything in life. Some of the seasons bring joy and happiness, like a new bride and groom, a new baby, graduating college, or that first job. These seasons bring joy and life and create a time to be celebrated. We love times like this and pray they never end. These periods in life tend to fade quickly and return more slowly as we age.

Then, unfortunately comes the season of weeping and tears. The joy and happiness fade and are replaced by heartache and dismay. Sickness, mourning, death, loss of employment, divorce, and uncountable other seasons of weeping and tears. It seems that these seasons will never end, that fullness of life will not return, and that we have been abandoned in our life and faith. We try to stay encouraged, knowing that what we are walking through is just a season.

My friend, my prayer is that you find encouragement and strength this day regardless of the season of life you are in. The Bible reminds us that we will experience these seasons. We will laugh, cry, weep, sing, dance, slumber, wage war, have peace, be silent, speak, hate, love, kill, harm, and heal. But in the end, my friend, we stand victorious, knowing that our God who created us is powerful and all-sufficient. Lean on Jesus today; tell Him your heart's story. Let Jesus comfort you in your season of weeping and tears and give Him praise and worship in your season of joy and happiness. God is a faithful God. Stay true to Him.

Prayer

God, cause me to stay committed to You in my times of weeping and tears and to praise You in my times of joy and happiness. I know You have a perfect plan for my life. Thank You, Jesus. Amen.

What's in a Name?

Main Text

John 5:24: "Very truly I tell you, whoever hears my word and believes him who sent me has eternal life and will not be judged but has crossed over from death to life."

Meditation

Your name is very important. That's why parents spend hours, days, and even weeks researching names and their meanings and origins. They see what they sound like with the first and last name put together, they think about how long the name is, and they consider a variety of other personal likes and dislikes. Once you have been given a birth name, it will follow you forever. It is interesting to learn that in the past twenty years, the most common boys' name was Jacob; in fact, this was true in fourteen of the past twenty years. Interesting to note that Jacob, as we know him from a biblical perspective, was a liar, a cheat, a flawed man, and even at times an idolater. Yet God described Himself as the "God of Abraham, the God of Isaac and the God of Jacob" in Exodus 3:6.

The most powerful name to consider as we examine names and their meaning is Jesus; *Iesous,* Greek or *Yesua,* Hebrew and Aramaic, meaning "the Lord is Salvation." We find the name of Jesus being first mentioned in Matthew 1:1. We often hear Jesus referred to as "Jesus Christ." Jesus Christ is not really a name, but rather a name and a title. It would be like saying, "Jesus, PhD." We add the title "Christ" to Jesus' name to identify Him as the promised Messiah. *Christ* comes from the Greek word *Christos,* which translates to *Messiah,* the "anointed one."

Talk about the meaning in a name. Every other name suddenly pales of comparison, doesn't it?

We use the name of Jesus Christ to bring meaning to our Redeemer and what He has done for us. Jesus died for us, rose from death triumphal, and lives today so that we might have life in Him and through His powerful name. The name Jesus brings many different associated meanings to mind such as life, victory, power, resurrection, joy, peace, strength, authority, and trust. The list of adjectives that we could use to describe the person of Jesus is endless. I am confident today that the name of Jesus, "the Lord is salvation," is the most powerful and influential name ever! As you search the meaning of your name, keep in mind the significance of our Lord and Savior, Jesus Christ.

Prayer

Jesus, You are my Savior, my anointed one. Thank You that Your name is powerful and supreme and that You gave me hope for a bright future with You. Amen.

Treetops

Main Text

2 Samuel 5:23–24: "So David inquired of the LORD, and he answered, 'Do not go straight up, but circle around behind them and attack them in front of the poplar trees. As soon as you hear the sound of marching in the tops of the poplar trees, move quickly, because that will mean the LORD has gone out in front of you to strike the Philistine army.'"

Meditation

The world's largest tree is located in California's Sequoia National Park. The tree, named General Sherman, is 52,500 cubic feet in size and stands 275 feet tall. General Sherman is estimated to be over two thousand years old, based on the tree ring counts. General Sherman is considered a mere baby tree with the oldest tree ever on record being 3,220 years old. In 1879, General Sherman was given its named after the American Civil War general William Tecumseh Sherman, who was famous for his ability to lead and his larger-than-life personality. Appropriately named, wouldn't you agree?

I really enjoy reading Bible stories to learn how God orchestrates events, often in unusual ways and through unique means. Take for instance the story where God used trees to help David win a battle. The story goes like this. It seems that King David was continuously waging war against the Philistines. We read in 2 Samuel 5 of such an account. David had just been appointed king when he received word through his "secret service" men that the Philistines were about to attack. David masterminded a plan to attack the Philistines quickly before they had the opportunity to mobilize and attack him. Before David enacted his plan, he went to the Lord and asked if he should attack. He actually asked the Lord if He would deliver him from the Philistines. God's response was that he should attack and that God would deliver him. David obeyed and the victory was his.

The Philistines were clearly not pleased by David's surprise attack and soon planned a second attack, of which David also received word. David again inquired of the Lord. The Lord said, "Do not go straight up, but circle around behind them and attack them in front of the poplar trees. As soon as you hear the sound of marching in the tops of the poplar trees, move quickly, because that will mean the LORD has gone out in front of you to strike the Philistine army" (2 Samuel 5:23–24). Second battle, second win, because David was obedient to the Lord.

The Lord works in and through people and things to bring victory to our lives. Just as the Lord used the treetops as a sign to David, He uses signs throughout our lives. Are you watching and listening for the signs God has placed before you? Open your spiritual eyes and ears that you might receive God's direction. God may just use the trees to help deliver you.

Prayer

Father, give me the ability to hear and see what You have for me. Let me seek You through people and yes, even the trees. Amen.

Caught You

Main Text

Acts 16:28: "But Paul shouted, 'Don't harm yourself! We are all here!'"

Meditation

"Women Arrested for Battery and Assault with Butter." "Man on Parole, Text Parole Officer Asking If He Had 'Weed' for Sale." "Robber Gets Tired, Lays Down for a Nap and Is Caught." Headlines like these make us all laugh, or at least shake our heads in disbelief. These were stories about actual arrests that were recently made by law enforcement. Some of the arrests seem so unbelievable they make us wonder what our society has come to.

The Bible records some crazy arrest stories as well. I can see the headlines now. "Jail Break! Paul and Silas Freed, but Don't Run." The story went like this. Paul, Silas, and a group of friends were traveling and preaching. They encountered a lady who was a fortuneteller. This lady continuously followed Paul and Silas, shouting behind them, "These men are servants of the Most High God, who are telling you the way to be saved" (Acts 16:17). She would not stop, no matter what Paul and Silas did. Finally, in an act of desperation, Paul could not take her actions anymore and commanded, "In the name of Jesus Christ I command you to come out of her!" (v. 18). At once the spirit within this woman left. The owner of this fortuneteller immediately became angered, as Paul had taken from him the way in which he made a living using this woman's fortunetelling skills.

Paul and Silas were arrested, beaten, and thrown into prison. That night Paul and Silas began to sing and praise God. Really, they began to sing and praise God? That certainly seems like odd behavior for folks who've just been put in prison. As they continued to sing and praise God, the miraculous occurred. An earthquake, so strong that it shook the prison, caused the doors to rip open and the chains to be loosened from their hands and feet. The prison guard came in haste, filled with dread that all the prisoners had fled. In the guard's moment of fear, he began to draw his sword to take his life, knowing the king would command his death for letting prisoners escape. He was stopped by Paul and Silas, who cried out to him, "Don't harm yourself! We are all here!" The guard fell to his knees and said, "Sirs, what must I do to be saved?" (vv. 28–30).

Paul and Silas are examples for us of God's ability to perform the seemingly impossible. In prison, against all odds, God shook the prison through an earthquake, Paul and Silas were set free, they didn't run, they shared the gospel, and God changed the life of the prison guard.

What is your prison? Where can you serve to share the good news? What crazy and wild story do you have to share about your redemption through God's love and grace in your life? You may be facing a situation that seems impossible to overcome. Sing and praise God; it may be your "jailbreak" that leads to your freedom and the salvation of others.

Prayer

Father, thank You that You have freed me. Let me be like Paul and Silas, who prayed and praised You when they were in trouble. I ask that You give me the boldness to stand for You in difficult times. Amen.

Persistence

Main Text

Luke 18:7: "And will not God bring about justice for his chosen ones, who cry out to him day and night? Will he keep putting them off?"

Meditation

Did you play a game called Persistence with your parents when you were growing up? Doesn't sound familiar? The game goes something like this: As a child you wanted a certain toy from the store or a chocolate treat and your parents repeatedly said no. You asked time and again, and they said no time and again. That did not stop you, however, because in your mind you knew that if you asked long enough and were persistent, you could eventually wear them down. We have all been on both the giving and receiving sides of this game. My experience with the game Persistence is that if you ask long enough, you are going to get exactly what you want. It's proven: persistence works.

Jesus talked about persistence in prayer and told a parable in Luke 18 about a woman who was relentless in her quest to seek justice from her enemy. Time and again this woman presented herself before the judge and begged him to provide justice to her and punish those who sought to harm her. Each time she came before the judge, the judge refused her request. Time and time again, the woman made her petition known. Finally, the day arrived that the woman made her petition once again and the judge granted her plea for justice. It was the woman's persistence that drove the judge to say, "Because this widow keeps bothering me, I will see that she gets justice, so that she won't eventually come and attack me!" (v. 5).

Jesus used this parable to instruct His disciples, as well as us, to be persistent in prayer. We are to bring our request before our heavenly Father, letting Him know what we need. Although in our minds, our prayers may sound like a broken record of the same request, Scripture is clear that we are to continue earnestly in prayer. Although God may not answer our prayers on our time schedule, I believe, and Scripture supports, that He is a just and fair God and answers our prayers according to what He knows is best for us. "And will not God bring about justice for his chosen ones, who cry out to Him day and night?" (v. 7). My friend, I am convinced that God does hear our prayers. I am also convinced that God answers our prayers. It may be, though, that we simply do not like His answers. Be persistent today. God is waiting to hear from you.

Prayer

Father, I know You hear my prayers. Please take my persistent prayer and answer it according to Your will. Cause me to be accepting of Your response. Amen.

Oh Be Careful Little Mouth

Main Text

Ephesians 4:29: "Do not let any unwholesome talk come out of your mouths, but only what is helpful for building others up according to their needs, that it may benefit those who listen."

Meditation

There is an old catchy song that we learned as children that goes like this: "Oh be careful little eyes what you see. Oh be careful little eyes what you see. There's a Father up above and He's looking down in love, so be careful little eyes what you see." The last verse of this song says, "Oh be careful little mouth what you say. Oh be careful little mouth what you say. There's a Father up above and He's looking down in love, so be careful little mouth what you say." This tune will play over and over in your mind today because you cannot read these words without the song's melody getting stuck in your head.

The words of this simple little song are so true and carry such power in them. Our eyes and our mouths can easily get us into trouble if we let them. Too often it is easy to become judgmental and accusing of others. We judge looks, attitudes, beliefs, personal dislikes, circumstances, dress, body piercings, and tattoos. When we judge, we gossip. We take our judgments and arrogance and use hurtful words that deeply scar those we love, care about, and respect. When we prematurely decide what is right and wrong, we may accuse and blame based on unknown facts. Words cannot be taken back. Once spoken, words live on in our minds. Words have the ability to build us up or tear us down. Gossip tears us down. It destroys and eats away at our mental emotions and builds wedges in relationships.

Ephesians 4:29 says, "Do not let any unwholesome talk come out of your mouths, but only such what is helpful for building others up according to their needs, that it may benefit those who listen." Before we speak, we need to realize the impact our words may have on others. We need to focus on building up others in Jesus' name and setting gossip aside. My prayer for you today is that you build someone up by using words of affirmation through God's grace. Remember, "Oh be careful little mouth what you say. Oh be careful little mouth what you say. There's a Father up above and He's looking down in love, so be careful little mouth what you say."

Prayer

God, help me control my tongue. Let no gossip or ill words come from my mouth. Amen.

Making the Cut

Main Text

John 15:16: "You did not choose me, but I chose you and appointed you so that you might go and bear fruit—fruit that will last—and so that whatever you ask in my name the Father will give you."

Meditation

Your pulse is racing. A bead of sweat begins to run down the side of your face. You fear that you may be the last kid standing as the team captains pick their teammates. I hated that feeling as a kid. I still dislike that feeling as an adult; we all do. No one wants to be last. We all want to be chosen at the beginning, not the end. Society has engrained in us that being first is most important. Look at professional sports. The best, the fastest, the strongest, the most highly paid all get chosen first. In many aspects of life, if we are not selected first, we think we have failed.

As team captain, I believe God chose an all-star team. He might not have selected the fastest, or the most qualified, instead He chose based on the willingness and commitment of their hearts. Consider the starting lineup. God chose Mary to be the mother of Jesus, the Savior of the world. Did He choose the right woman? Humble, lowly, and meek with an obedient heart. I'd say God chose the right woman. God chose Moses to lead His elect people to the promise land. Moses, if you recall, said, "Who am I that I should go to Pharaoh and bring the Israelites out of Egypt?" (Exodus 3:11). Moses lacked self-confidence and was a poor communicator, but God chose him. God chose David, a shepherd boy, to be Israel's second and greatest king. David went from herding sheep in the pasture to occupying the royal throne. God chose the unknown, lightweight Elijah the prophet to destroy Baal. Elijah prayed to God for help, and God sent fire down from heaven to demonstrate His power and confirm the message Elijah was trying to deliver to the people. God chose Esther, a nobody, to become the queen who helped save her people.

Incredible stories, aren't they? These were ordinary people who ended up having extraordinary events play out through their lives. I doubt that any of God's team had any idea what they had signed up for. They were hand-selected by God for His purpose and in His time. My friend, I believe that God has hand-selected you as well. You may not know it or want it, but you're in the game. You may not be the next King David or Queen Esther, but God has His perfect plan in store for you. Ponder that thought today as you examine your life. Where has God placed you that you need to rise to the occasion and "knock it out of the park"?

Prayer

God, I know You have selected me to accomplish great things. I may not know what these things are, but I ask that You clearly direct me to the things You have for me to accomplish for You. Amen.

Day 88

Beginning or End?

Main Text

Revelation 1:8: "'I am the Alpha and the Omega,' says the Lord God, 'who is, and who was, and who is to come, the Almighty.'"

Meditation

Our current English alphabet has twenty-six letters. But the English alphabet did not always contain twenty-six letters. The origin of the alphabet and writing system we know today actually goes back to the consonantal writing system (only consonants were written and vowels were left out) that was created for Semitic languages native to West Asia, or more commonly known as the Middle East. The idea of letters, shapes, and symbols were developed by the Egyptians and initially designed for a single people group. The idea of symbols and drawings that delivered meaning quickly spread to nearby neighboring people groups to the east and north. As time passed, the use of a standardized symbol and drawing system developed into the modern-day English alphabet we know and use today.

God declared He is the beginning and the end, the A through Z if you will. There is coming a day when the beginning, alpha, will meet the end, omega. It will be a reunion in the sky when Jesus Himself returns to earth to take home those who have committed themselves to Him. Scripture is clear that God has sent His only Son, Jesus, to the earth to be the Deliverer, the salvation for mankind. When life is over on earth, we will be taken to heaven. Revelation tells us that "He is coming with the clouds," and "every eye will see him, even those who pierced him" (1:7). Imagine the day Jesus will appear riding a white stallion through the clouds to take us away to heaven. If you have ever watched a movie about the coming of Jesus, you will have seen all the glitz and glamor that Hollywood can create to depict Jesus' second coming. I am here to tell you that Hollywood's version of Jesus' return is a mere glimpse of the real act. When Jesus descends from heaven, it will be the final scene, uncut, raw, and real.

Do you have your bags packed to make the journey to heaven? Be ready to take the trip. Revelation 1:8 says, "'I am the Alpha and the Omega,' says the Lord God, 'who is, and who was, and who is to come, the Almighty.'"

Prayer

God, thank You for preparing the way for me to go to heaven and for giving Your own son for me. What a day it will be when I see my Jesus face-to-face. Amen.

Day 89

Color Your World

Main Text

1 Peter 3:15: "But in your hearts revere Christ as Lord. Always be prepared to give an answer to everyone who asks you to give the reason for the hope you have. But do this with gentleness and respect."

Meditation

Manatee, razzmatazz, thistle, inch worm, and outer space. Any guess what the connection is between these words? If you guessed colors found in a box of Crayola crayons, congratulations. I have no idea what any of these colors look like. Crayola reports that their assortment of crayons has 120 different colors to choose from. I want to know what happened to the colors I grew up with. Colors like blue, purple, green, red, and yellow? You know, the colors that we all know and can appreciate.

The world has become complex and confusing right down to the color choices found in a box of Crayola crayons. Jesus calls us to be different and to make the right choices. Being different does not mean being weird or unapproachable; rather, it means sharing Jesus' love with others. We are called to be prepared in our belief of Jesus, to stand ready to defend our faith. First Peter 3:15 says, "But in your hearts revere Christ as Lord. Always be prepared to give an answer to anyone who asks you to give the reason for the hope that you have. But do this with gentleness and respect."

We can be prepared to defend our faith by reading our Bible and praying daily. We can uphold our faith by doing the right things when others do wrong. We can share, give, and encourage others. Whatever we do, we need to be prepared to share in the love, grace, and gentleness that Jesus instills in us. Pushing or scorning someone for not believing in Jesus only drives them away. There is an old cliché that says, "You can catch more bees with honey." Be the fragrance of Jesus and share His love, standing ready to defend your Savior, but do it in a spirit of grace.

So, back to our box of crayons. If I were to ask you what color best describes you, what color would you choose? Color your world today with the love of Jesus.

Prayer

Father, thank You for giving me color in my life. Let me stand ready to defend You and represent You in a way that is pleasing to You. Amen.

Day 90

Cost Benefit

Main Text

Romans 6:23: "For the wages of sin is death, but the gift of God is eternal life in Christ Jesus our Lord."

Meditation

If I had the ability to grant you one wish, what would you wish for? Fame, fortune, health, a family, a career, a new car, faith? What one thing do you want more than anything else? That's a big decision, isn't it? I am not sure what I would choose either. We tend not to look at life in terms of wishes or gifts that can be given to us. Instead, we have determined in our mind that we need to work hard in order to get ahead and achieve what we want. We need to do it on our own, forging the way before us in order to succeed. I believe if you ask anyone to reflect back on their life and asked what one thing they would change if they could, it would be to work less and enjoy family and friends more.

God offers the best gift at no cost: eternal life through Jesus. It is yours, if you choose. Okay, let's be honest. There is a cost of living for Jesus. There are strings attached. There are conditions. Not what you wanted to hear, I know. When you break it down, you will see there is a significant cost in living for Jesus. God asks that we surrender things that cause us to stumble, but from a worldly standpoint are hard to give up. Perhaps it is drunkenness, gambling, weekend parties, crude language and jokes, promiscuous actions, or other worldly things that get in your way of following Jesus. You see, all of these things only provide contentment for a season, then they fade, leaving you longing for something more, something different. The trade-off for the cost of serving Jesus is the fact that we can live a redemptive life in the freedom, joy, happiness, love, peace, strength, contentment, assurance, and power of our Savior without regrets. A commitment to Jesus is high, but the cost of not committing is higher.

What choice have you made? What choice should you make? My prayer for you is that Jesus meets you where you are and that His peace overpowers your heart. Live in the freedom of Jesus; make the sacrifice to live for Him.

Prayer

God, thank You for sending Your Son, Jesus, for me. Thank You for causing me to accept the gift of life eternal. I know there is a cost to follow You, but the cost far outweighs the alternatives of a life without You. Amen.

Scripture Reference

Day	Scripture	Day	Scripture
1	2 Samuel 22:2–3	20	1 Samuel 17:4
2	Isaiah 41:13	21	John 4:7
3	Mark 12:42	22	Luke 8:45–46
4	Proverbs 3:6	23	Philippians 1:21
5	Romans 5:5	24	Philippians 4:6
6	1 Corinthians 1:9	25	Exodus 2:7
7	Mark 4:5	26	Ephesians 1:19
8	2 Corinthians 5:1	27	1 Corinthians 9:24
9	Psalm 78:14	28	Galatians 3:26–27
10	Titus 2:11–12	29	Exodus 3:3
11	Matthew 6:26	30	Matthew 25:13
12	Psalm 51:10	31	Matthew 12:36–37
13	James 1:12	32	2 Corinthians 2:15
14	2 Thessalonians 3:3	33	Matthew 3:4
15	Revelation 21:18	34	Genesis 1:25
16	Mathew 14:25–26	35	Nehemiah 9:6
17	Isaiah 12:2	36	1 Corinthians 15:57
18	Colossians 3:23	37	Mark 2:11–12
19	Joshua 6:5	38	Matthew 5:8
39	John 3:16	60	Hebrews 12:1–2
40	Exodus 7:10	61	Ephesians 2:8–9

41	Psalm 119:103	62	Hebrews 11:1–2
42	Genesis 11:9	63	Jonah 1:11–12
43	Daniel 6:22	64	Acts 4:12
44	1 Kings 17:6	65	Numbers 27:18
45	Isaiah 40:31	66	2 Chronicles 6:19
46	John 14:6	67	Isaiah 30:21
47	Psalm 62:6	68	1 Corinthians 15:52
48	2 Timothy 3:16–17	69	Psalm 90:12
49	Psalm 19:1	70	Genesis 6:13
50	Romans 10:15	71	Mark 4:39–40
51	Psalm 139:14	72	Matthew 7:25
52	Numbers 22:28	73	Matthew 13:33
53	Exodus 14:15–16	74	1 John 5:14–15
54	1 John 1:9	75	Psalm 33:2
55	John 16:33	76	Job 11:7
56	Mark 13:32	77	John 13:5
57	Psalm 148:2	78	Nahum 1:7
58	2 Samuel 7:28	79	1 Timothy 6:18–19
59	John 8:12	80	1 Corinthians 11:25–26
81	Ecclesiastes 3:1	86	Ephesians 4:29
82	John 5:24	87	John 15:16
83	2 Samuel 5:23–24	88	Revelation 1:8
84	Acts 16:28	89	1 Peter 3:15
85	Luke 18:7	90	Romans 6:23

About the Author

Todd Diedrich is a full-time senior business executive in central Wisconsin, where he is active in a variety of community- and church-related activities. Todd is a licensed pastor with the Assemblies of God affiliation. Most notable, Todd serves as the missions director in the church he attends. Todd is involved in leading mission's initiatives to help fund-raise and provide resources to missionaries serving abroad.

Todd devotes time to public speaking, providing leadership training, and conducting strategic-planning sessions for businesses, government units, schools, and not-for-profit organizations across the Midwest. Additionally, Todd is an adjunct instructor at his local community college, where he teaches in the business department. Todd and his wife, Julene, reside in central Wisconsin and enjoy traveling and spending time with family and friends.

Printed in the United States
By Bookmasters